Punk. No One is Innocent

Art – Style – Revolt

KUNSTHALLE wien

 Verlag für moderne Kunst Nürnberg

Content

Foreword

Gerald Matt

Let us put our trust in the eternal spirit which destroys and annihilates only because it is the unsearchable and eternally creative source of all life. The passion for destruction is also a creative passion.

Michael Bakunin, *Reaction in Germany* (1842)

No One is Innocent – because everyone knew. History was being made, but not progress. In the late 1970s, the so-called developed world had manoeuvred itself into an economic and social dead end: in Britain, unemployment was on the rise, and with it the sense of political frustration. The triumphal celebration of the Queen's Silver Jubilee was an all too obvious ploy to divert attention away from pressing social problems. The United States were still paralysed by Watergate and the aftermath of the Vietnam War, with Ronald Reagan already saddling up to ride into the neo-liberal age beyond the sunset. And Germany found itself on permanent alert: the hijacking by Palestinians of a German plane at Mogadishu airport; the kidnapping and murder of Hans Martin Schleyer by the Baader-Meinhof Gang; the mysterious deaths of leading Red Army Fraction terrorists at Stuttgart's Stammheim jail; and at every newsstand, a poster with mug shots of terrorists – Wanted, Dead or Alive!

Just ten years after the optimistic mood of the "Summer of Love," the generation of May 1968 was already part of the establishment, the hippies were an institution, the flower child had become a fashion industry staple. And the world found itself in a state of shock, repression and trauma. These were the social conditions under which a new subculture set out to conquer first the headlines and then the minds of an army of disorientated young people. Punk was "musique d'ameublement," but not the way Erik Satie meant it. Instead, the idea was to furnish totally devastated mental interiors with cryptic visual and acoustic signs. "There was a black hole at the heart of the Sex Pistols' music," wrote Greil Marcus in his brilliant *Lipstick Traces*, "a wilful lust for the destruction of values that no one could be comfortable with."

As an art institution, following the guitar exhibition *Go Johnny Go!* (2003) and the *Summer of Love* show (2006), we are interested in Punk less as a musical phenomenon than as a gesture of negation – as a door of perception through which one enters a realm of encoded messages: signal to noise.

Punk took the texts and ideologemes of a dubious structure of power and hope and of an exhausted hippie and student protest counterculture, chopped them up, and put them together in a new order, entirely in keeping with Bertolt Brecht's claim that: "What is 'natural' must contain the force of the disruptive." In this sense, the chaos movement started by Malcolm McLaren and Vivienne Westwood at 430 King's Road was a zero point of popular culture – a blank canvas on which a new generation of artists, musicians, filmmakers, graphic artists and fashion designers made their mark, to challenge social and political power, and to reveal the construction of meaning as a swindle.

At the same time, the field was opened up for new connections and synaptic leaps between artistic styles and individuals who may have been far apart in terms of both geography and mentality, but who nonetheless spoke the same language. Such lines can be drawn, for example, from the ritualized masturbation fantasies of Vito Acconci in the New York of 1972 and the revolting scenarios staged in the milieu of the Berlin band Einstürzende Neubauten; and from Lynda Benglis' dildo photograph in *Artforum* magazine 1974 to the deconstructive engagement with pornography by the British group COUM Transmissions/ Throbbing Gristle. "The moment of true poetry," wrote Situationist Guy Debord, "brings the unpaid debts of history back into play." In this sense, Punk was perhaps the most successful debt collection enterprise in the history of popular culture. Focussing on the energy centres of New York, London and Berlin, the exhibition *Punk. No One is Innocent* shows how variously and yet how consistently Punk impacted on fine art, youth fashion and the symbols of revolt in different cultural spheres and socio-political milieus. Whereas in Britain it was mainly a phenomenon of fashion and style, generating a typical graphic look, in the United States and Germany there was from the outset a close link between artists and punks – many artists and avant-garde filmmakers like Jim Jarmusch, Wolfgang Müller, Alan Vega, Robert Longo, David Wojnarowicz and Salomé played in bands themselves. "It was dark, dangerous, exciting," said Laurie Anderson about New York in the late 1970s, "We knew we were creating a totally new scene. There were no limits and no categories. Everyone worked on everyone else's art and it didn't matter if it was dance or sculpture, painting or film. The definitions only came later, mostly from art schools that needed labels as names for their courses."

The exhibition *Punk. No One is Innocent* at Kunsthalle Wien shows that Punk was above all an artistic assertion of radicality which manifested itself as a semiotic revolution and which generated productive irritation with its do-it-yourself aesthetic. The optical traces of this long since historical movement made an impression on artistic forms of expression that persists to this day, also reaching the gallery and fashion mainstream via figures including Laurie Anderson and Vivienne Westwood.

I would like to take this opportunity to thank all those who helped to turn a vague idea into a project that will hopefully provoke some enjoyable arguments. First, my thanks go to curator Thomas Mießgang, who was an eye-witness as a member of the moderately successful new wave band Radical Chic, and curatorial assistant Synne Genzmer, who was born when Punk was already almost over but who more than made up for this in terms of hard work. Thanks are also due to Sigrid Mittersteiner (production), Claudia Bauer (press and marketing) and Johnny Diboky (technician) – the reliable Kunsthalle team who once again remained realistic and made the impossible happen. I am very grateful to Jon Savage, Glenn O'Brien and Wolfgang Müller for their informative essays on Punk and art in London, New York and Berlin – lively accounts of these three vibrant scenes from people who were there. Not least, thanks are due to the artists and all those who loaned works, without whose cooperation and support the show would not have been possible. Thanks also to Verlag für moderne Kunst Nürnberg for its cooperation on realizing the catalogue, and to Dieter Auracher for the graphic design.

ANARCHY IN THE U.K.

No1

20p

SEX PISTOLS

Jamie Reid, Sophie Richmond, Vivienne Westwood, *Anarchy In The U.K. Sex Pistols*, No.1, 1976

i am an antichrist
i am an anarchist
don't know what i want
but i know how to get it
i wanna destroy the passerby

'cause i wanna be anarchy
no dogsbody

Anarchy In The U.K., Sex Pistols

No One is Innocent

Chaos and enlightenment, violence and passion, fashion and despair – what is left of Punk and what has disappeared into the black hole

Thomas Mießgang

Old oaths, carrying forgotten curses, which themselves contained buried wishes, were pressed into seven-inch pieces of plastic as a bet that someone would listen, that someone would decipher codes the speakers themselves didn't know they were transmitting.

Greil Marcus, *Lipstick Traces*

What was the year when Punk broke through the surface? Was it 1976, when Johnny Rotten, bent over the microphone and laughing jeeringly, like an adolescent hunchback of Notre Dame on British television, declaimed his legendary declaration of war on the world: "I am an antichrist, I am an anarchist"? Or one year earlier, when Patti Smith, shuddering with the holy spirit of Rimbaud, marked the start of her subjective search for the Grail with the symbolic elimination of all Christian values: "Jesus Christ died for somebody's sins but not mine"? Perhaps it was as early as 1956, the year when Elvis Presley unfettered his body in the Milton Berle Show like a Rock 'n' Roll Houdini and let his legs jerk spastically as if they didn't belong to the rest of his physical appearance? "That was the dance everyone forgot," was the comment back then of the Rockabilly singer Butch Hancock: "It was the dance that was so strong it took an entire civilization forget it. And ten seconds to remember it."[1] A "Hound Dog" on the way to the Hell of desire. Or to the heaven. The truth is in the eye of the observer, conveyed by his or her socio-political status. Punk is a multi-coded project of unreconciliation: on the one hand, a manifestation determined by music, fashion, art and the history of style, which had its greatest symbol-political and geographic extension in the years from 1976 to 1978. On the other hand, a fundamental attitude of negation, whose historical traces and metaphoric charge-energies can be pursued to the "illegitimate" avant-gardes of the 20th century (Dadaism, Lettrism, Situationism) and beyond them as well (the *poètes maudits* of

the *fin de siècle* and, as an ultimate consequence, even heretics in the Middle Ages) – as Greil Marcus has done in his standard work *Lipstick Traces*. The term itself can be traced back etymologically to its first use in Shakespeare's play *Measure for Measure*, where a prostitute is characterised as a "punk." More relevant in our connection is Frank Zappa's song *Flower Punk* from 1968 – a piece of anti-hippie rhetoric typical of its time from the "progressive" camp – and the phenomenon of garage punk bands, who celebrated lo-fi sound bruitism at the periphery of pop culture using limited means of production. Consciousness-narrowing and structural minimalism as an acne-infected contrast programme to the proto-spiritual large acoustic formats painted by bands like Grateful Dead and Quicksilver Messenger Service. In garage sound, with its spooky harmonica effects, a rhythm reduced to the simplest Big Beat and distorted guitar clusters swinging unstably between chord and noise, a great deal can already be found which was to become a pop-cultural conflagration ten years later as "Punk 77." But the phenomenon as we understand and present it in the exhibition *No One is Innocent* can be interpreted less as a musical generation than as a metaphor of a deletion, a stylistic device, which activated a sensory destruction programme in the moment of its metaphorical presence, throwing the grammar of old traditional pop cultures and socio-political systems into confusion, to a much greater extent than its authors intended. "It is just a pop song, a would-be, has-been hit record, a cheap commodity," wrote Greil Marcus on *Anarchy In The U.K.* by the Sex Pistols. "And yet the voice telling that carries it remains something new in rock 'n' roll, which is to say something new in postwar popular culture: a voice that denied all social facts, and in that denial affirmed that every-

---

1   Butch Hancock, quoted from Greil Marcus, *Lipstick Traces. A Secret History of the Twentieth Century*, Cambridge, Mass., 2003, p. 126.
In the subsequent Ed Sullivan Show only a waist-up version of Elvis was to be seen, because those responsible for the program did not want to, or could not impose the anarchic lust of a body liberated from puritanical body domestication rituals on the American TV family.

thing was possible. It remains new because rock 'n' roll has not caught up with it."[2]

"Nothing is true, everything is allowed." – The old Situationist proverb was connected to amplifiers, the body was sung electrically and at the same time language was hacked up into stuttering in the face of the saint or the monster. Never could the question "Who broke my song so badly, Ma?" be asked as honestly as in the world-historical moment when the world as we knew it was once more illuminated in flash of perception before it was deleted from the hard disk. Over and out.

The fact that it came back a little later as a caricature and sharper vision of itself is another story and means only that symbol-political revolutions that refuse to set up hegemonies with traditional means, such as state apparatus, military, and police, can only be grasped as transitory moments, little epiphanies, which work more inwardly than outwardly. On the other hand, however, they mean more *in the long run* than the shifts of power, lacing in mystery, of traditional political upheavals and preserve the true Mystery of the desire for the impossible which creates its own idioms and platforms on the boulevards of adolescent excess in the forms of glossolalia, style war and theatre of cruelty.

Rock 'n' roll revolution as a new cartography in psychogeography, sound politics as the frame of action for a spirit that always negates and, in its annihilatory consistency, at the same time creates the conditions for areas of possibility on the far side of the spectacular boredom of eventless event-milieus.

Music may have been implemented in 1976/77 by money-hungry impresarios as a carrier medium or, if one will, as a gun carriage from which Punk was shot into the media universe and the public debating arena, but a large number of subsystems had to work together to make possible the "deep impact" of the last global youth movement, which was more and wanted to be more than acoustic furniture in teenager bedrooms: advertising art, fashion, mass media, art and politics that gladly let themselves be provoked and struck back in a predictable way.

There is something of a consensus in the relevant reference literature (Greil Marcus, Jon Savage, Simon Reynolds, Dick Hebdige, Simon Frith et al.), that punk-like subcultures and style models were moved forward in time – the sufficiently known genealogy of The Velvet Underground through MC 5, Iggy Pop & The Stooges to the New York Dolls, with a few side-trips to the Glam of Roxy Music and Co – but that the kind of Punk that is associated with the eyes of Johnny Rotten staring in a paranoid way into the abyss embodied a different existential density, another degree of hardness in the production of chaos.

The conditions for an uprising of signs were not bad: the USA still traumatised by Watergate and the endless Vietnam war, England shattered by IRA terror and kicked into the off-side of the global economy after years of financial mismanagement by the state and Berlin in the shadow of the wall still quite willing to take part in a pretty dance on the volcano. Hippie culture and May 68 were now only a distant afterglow on the horizon of utopia. The revolt had split into little skirmishes in the trenches of secondary battlefields (splinters of East German socialism) or had subsided into an "armed struggle" without any basis in the population, in other words: terrorism. In the face of the general feeling that something had been promised ten years earlier but the promise had not been kept, people like the music manager and Situationism-inclined spitfire Malcolm McLaren, the graphic artist Jamie Reid and the fashion designer Vivenne Westwood made a beginning. A clothing shop called Sex (later Seditionaries) on the King's Road in London became the headquarters of a project worked out on the drawing board for the revaluation of all values. The semiotic guerilla used T-shirts as the carrier medium for puzzling messages and shocking images, making S/M clothing the illegitimate covering for the everyday performance in the city's municipal area, and McLaren, who had been a failure shortly before in this very city as the manager of the New York Dolls cast an anti-boy group with dyed spiked hair from the workers in the Sex shop and young men who lounged about at the entrance. He called them the "Sex Pistols" and used their working-

---

2   Marcus 2003, p. 2.

class appeal, not only to shock TV moderators,[3] record companies and a discreetly shivering public but also to attack the petrified English class system. That was détournement in its classical situationist meaning: an ambush with the aim of mastering the familiar in order to change it into the other, or, as Guy Debord formulated it: to bring oil to a place where there was fire. The original intention of the British Punk cell may have been to gain "cash from chaos," but soon something quite different came of it: a whirl of signs and emblems, a cacophony of ideologically formed meanings that were carried into the annihilation of meaning with destructive furore.[4]

According to the vision of Malcolm McLaren, Punk was designed to be a big "NO!", which was always in danger of slipping into pure nihilism. The emblematic legend of Sid and Nancy laid down for all times that consumption of too many things, whether as a gesture of denial or from an impulse to self-destruction, ends with one falling into the black hole that was always at the heart of Punk, consumed oneself. But wherever Punk worked – and that was always in places one had formerly known nothing about or that they even existed – it succeeded in cutting through the vocal cords of any authorised spokesperson who defended the politics of boredom and depression,[5] in order to reach a condition of spiritual anarchy that withdrew from ideological codification and undermine the apparent rationality of the "Society of Specta-

cle" in cursing, madness and excess.[6] Punk was thus more like an aggregate condition of existence than a form of cultural expression. It used pop music as a preferred vehicle because that was simply the medium with which teenagers could be reached directly without digressions, but it was not limited to that. Blixa Bargeld of the band Einstürzende Neubauten once said that he was on the path towards becoming a painter when he came to music more or less by chance. The need for expression looks for its own channels, the will to contradict had to destroy the language that society, over which the brain police exercised hegemony, used to talk in autoerotic monologues, and reconstruct it from stammering, onomatopoetic meta-lyrics and regressive baby-babble. It was a matter of an idiomatic style between dream and reality, whose meaning lay in its self-consumption, and also of people who became the media for a matter about which, in most cases, they knew nothing.[7] But that is what is so wonderful about Punk: that in the heart of the cultural industry so vigorously combated by Adorno and Horkheimer, a mysterious sign emerged that tells what it is like to be lost to the world and simultaneously to work on the becoming of a new subjectivity while in a subjective reverie. For the Punk that interests us – the moment when Johnny Rotten asked the public, at the last concert of the Sex Pistols in the Winterland of San Francisco: "Ever get the feeling you've been cheated?" – is a becoming and not a being: "Become man – become woman – become animal," as we read in *A Thousand Plateaus* by Deleuze and Guattari. And until the signs had stabilised this process of the flowing of identities, sounds, metaphors and the borders between genders could continue. A quickstep of ambivalences: are they Nazis, because they wear swastikas, or are they juggling with ultra heavy signs without meaning or purpose? Can't they

3   On 1 December 1976 the Sex Pistols appeared with a group of fans on the BBC's *Bill Grundy Show*. The tipsy moderator provoked the band and was then smothered in wild insults ("Old fucker!"). The interview created a scandal in profoundly conservative England. Next day it was announced that Bill Grundy had been suspended for two weeks because of a "gross error of judgement." But the TV event also had consequences for the Sex Pistols: 13 von 19 tour appointments were cancelled, most commercial radio stations no longer placed Pistols records, big record shops stopped selling the single and EMI cancelled their contract with the Pistols. Cf. Al Spicer, *The Rough Guide to Punk*, London 2006, p. 29.

4   *Stop making Sense* was the name of a record and a concert film of the Talking Heads, who were accounted to a kind of Punk and No Wave scene in New York.

5   Arthur Rimbaud had already written in *Mauvais Sang*: "L'ennui n'est plus mon amour. Les rages, les débauches, la folie, dont je sais tous les élans et les désastres, – tout mon fardeau est déposé. Apprécions sans vertige l'étendu de mon innocence." Quoted from: www.mag4.net/Rimbaud/poesies/Sang. With a certain coerciveness, the poet of *Une saison en enfer* and the other French Symbolists became house-gods in particular of the New York Punk and No Wave lot. Patti Smith made literary performances under the title *Rock 'n' Rimbaud*; the poet and guitarist Tom Miller, who was to become famous with the band Television, called himself Tom Verlaine.

6   "The initial phase of the dominance of the economy over social life brought, in the definition of that human realisation, a clear degradation of *Being* into *Having*. The present phase of the total capture of social life by the accumulated results of the economy leads to a general shift from *Having* to *Appearing*, from which every real "Having" has to draw its immediate prestige and ultimate purpose. At the same time, every individual reality has become social, directly dependent on social power and formed by it. Only to the extent that it is not may it appear to be." Guy Debord, *Die Gesellschaft des Spektakels*, Berlin 1996, pp. 18 (Society of the Spectacle).

7   One may assume that Sid Vicious and Captain Sensible from The Damned read neither Guy Debord nor Tristan Tzara, let alone Isidore Isou.

tune their instruments, or don't they want to? On this point Wolfgang Müller from Die Tödliche Doris said: "The instruments are always in tune … a dilettante genius neither wants nor needs power over his instrument, or even dominate it. What he envisions is merely getting to know it in the hope that it will sometime speak of its own accord, intensely and concisely, showing the player who he is. The players themselves are mediums in the service of the instrument."[8] Become animal: infantilisation, regression, holy insanity, productive schizophrenia, in the excess of a physically exploding signifier: what post-structuralism set out to do, to repress good old critical theory in the lecture halls, goes together well with that shunting at the sign railway station, which Punk staged so brilliantly. It is just that the pop version of semantic confusion did not take place in the residual spaces of academic lecture halls and seminars but on the world stage of mass culture, and consequently had a very different effect on collective consciousness.

Just like Dadaism, Lettrism, Situationism, the early *Cahiers du Cinema* or, if one wants to go into the political arena, the Paris Commune or the French Revolution, Punk could only exist for the flicker of an eyelash as a nuisance factor in a social reality that went on reproducing itself without deeply questioning itself. One might locate this fermata in current operations in 1976, in 1974 when the Ramones – *Hey! Ho! Let's go!* – pulled on their leather jackets for the first time, or in, when Tristan Tzara, Marcel Janco, Hugo Ball and Co cried "Moo Moo" and "Mee-ow Mee-ow" in the Cabaret Voltaire in Zurich. The fact is that all the people who were illuminated by the spirit of holy Punk, didn't know at first what was happening to them and secondly, only after a long timespan, registered that everything had long been over.

The proverbial "I didn't really know it was happening" of sportspeople after winning a gold medal can be applied as much to the spooky beginning of Punk as to it lacklustre ending, which is to be set somewhere between 1978 and 1980, depending on one's historiographic preferences and geographic location. The careers had to go on of course, in spite of that. And so, for example, The Clash turned itself into a political contradiction ensemble with a relatively conventional socialist mindset with funk, rock, and reggae achses of distribution, and the Ramones kept travelling on the same track until their tyres had burnt down to the wheel-rim and the early death of almost all band members made future reunions impossible. Even the Sex Pistols are not too proud to chant "God save the Queen, she ain't no human being" at open-air festivals as a caricature of their younger selves. Even now at the 50-year jubilee of the coronation. This is the ultimate vaudevillisation of a phenomenon that was invented as a candle burning at both ends and now has the durability of atomic waste, which doesn't fit any final place of disposal.

In the course of three decades Punk has been packaged as a museum piece that is called up on the screen of collective memory clichés with the click of a mouse on certain indicators: Mohawk haircut, safety pin, badge with the slogan "No Future." The big tear in the collective brain has been sewn up again, the moment of excess has passed. The police are still carrying on, the rulers of states are still carrying on, the football players are still carrying on, the Neo-Nazis are still carrying on and, of course, Johnny Rotten is still carrying on (freely quoted from Rolf Dieter Brinkmann). What remains is the hangover after a big night out and the vaguely sensed silhouette of a dream: "To me the most haunting, prophetic outcry of the nineteenth century is Théophile Gautier's 'plutôt la barbaric que l'ennui!' (rather barbarism than boredom.) If we can come to understand the sources of that perverse longing, of that itch for chaos, we will be nearer to an understanding of our own state and of the relations of our condition to the accusing ideal of the past."[9]

9   George Steiner, *In Bluebeard's Castle,* Wien, Zürich 1991, p. 18.

8   Frank Apunkt Schneider, *Als die Welt noch unterging – Von Punk zu NDW,* Mainz 2007, p. 153.

In the City we can change our identities at will, as Dickens triumphantly proved over and over again in his fiction. Its discontinuity favours both instant heroes and instant villains impartially. The gaudy, theatrical nature of city life tends constantly to melodrama.

Jonathan Raban, *Soft City*

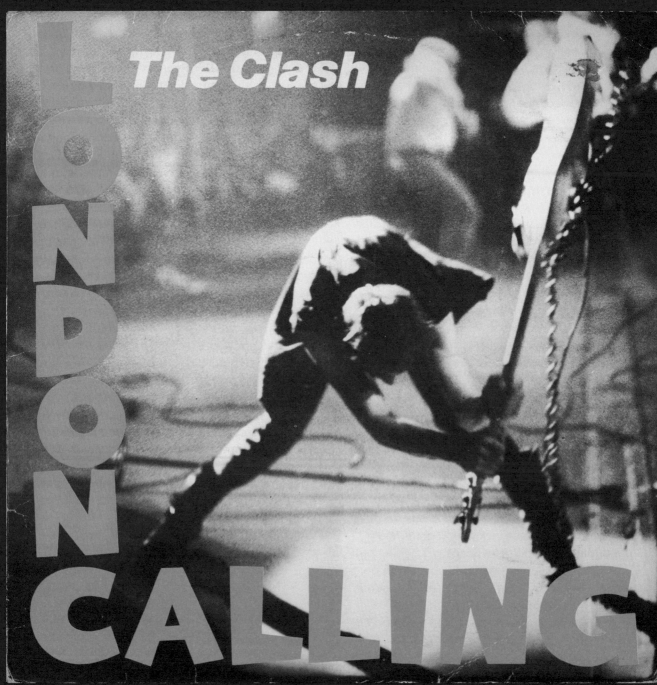

The Clash, *London Calling*, 1979

The city as a space for possibilities, urban settings as a test field for fluctuating constructions of identity, whose usefulness can be read in the disapproving or admiring eyes of passers-by: mirror phase as a formative for the ego-function. Leigh Bowery, the total work of art from Australia, who was lured to London by the Punk scene in 1980, played on this very keyboard: as a performer he linked with cross-gender dressing-up in direct line from David Bowie, Lindsay Kemp et al. as well as Gay Culture and the transvestite scene: with his face covered with black make-up as a parody of a blackface performance, his nipples pierced and hung with heavy chains, his voluminous body wrapped in nylon and foam, with frills a-flutter, and covered with a black-and-white spotted leopard skin. A transformer phenomenon between man and woman, vamp and vampire, reality and phantasmagoria. One of the most spectacular Bowery performances took place at the S/M night in the Bar Industria: with a lesbian girlfriend, this semanticist of the body stepped out in a Nazi uniform and managed to shock the gay community. The old game of breaching taboos in a little shop of horrors still worked perfectly, years after Siouxsie Sioux had laid down her swastika.

Leigh Bowery perfected visiting said clubs as a form of art. He practised a subjective-idiosyncratic form of Dérive, by travelling on the underground wearing costumes he had normally designed and cut in person, going shopping, strolling along the streets and challenging the aggression of his fellow-creatures with his "never seen before" look. A juggler with multiple roles, who played a guest part in the film *Epiphany* of Cerith Wyn Evans, collaborated with the dancer Michael Clark, and who appeared as a freely floating, allegorical figure in the play *Hey Luciani!* of the Fall singer Mark E. Smith. Most recently, he tried, without much success, to force his physical presence into a commercially sellable format with the band Minty. He didn't belong anywhere and yet was at home everywhere. That was "art on the far side of the gallery" even though Leigh Bowery was sometimes represented by Anthony d'Offay. This was the substrate of a highly stylised and excessive life-practice that led to a foreseeable early death and became a late echo of the unstable agglomerations of signs that Punk initiated.

As far as the pop subculture of the seventies was concerned, Leigh Bowery was a too-latecomer. The scene had long set the prefix "post" in front of the term "Punk" and had expanded in terms of style: New Romantic, Gothic Rock, Ska-Revival, the promiscuous milieu at the Blitz Club, Boy George as a consensual gay icon who could also be sold to the mainstream. Now, at last, clothes made the man, and the right hairstyle became a raison d'être. And so a circle was closed: even at the very beginning of Punk, the vestimentary code was dominant: before a band named Sex Pistols even existed and music was even thought of, Malcolm McLaren and Vivienne Westwood determined the operating temperature for the coming years with their fashion creations: they weaved slogans of the Spanish anarchist Buenaventura Durruti into their clothing and used sleeveless T-shirts as projection screens for excessive sexual fantasies and provocative, tasteless border-crossings: one might see a black football player with a powerful penis or the discomforting image of a twelve-year-old boy who was in the act of breathing out cigarette smoke – the template was a photo from *Boys Express*, a paedophile magazine from Essex with a small circulation. The interface for the mutual influence of fashion and graphic design was Jamie Reid, who derived his image inventions from the libertarian ideas of Charles Fourier and the anarchistic impulses of William Morris and Gerrard Winstanley. The graphic designer from Manchester, who designed the much-read situationist reader *Leaving the 20th Century*, became the visual stylist of the Punk scene, in particular because of his designs for Sex Pistols record covers. The collective memory is especially impressed with the single-cover to *God Save The Queen*: the eyes and mouth of the British Queen have the song title and the name of the group pasted over them – just like a kidnap victim. Reid used the same letters, cut from newspapers, to imitate the style of blackmail letters. The ideas behind this was Punk as an ambush on the consciousness of the masses. The public was symbolically turned into hostages and mistreated with demands, impertinence and optical shocks. The oblivious, solipsistic murmuring of power was suddenly confronted with an opposition that was able to capture the media for its own purposes and to infect the public arena of the streets, the means of transport, and points of assembly with the virus of irreconcilability. Loosely based on Debord, Punk wanted "to create confusion, without loving it." The rebellion of signs and the deconstruction of images, sounds and official declarations of enclosed dominance idioms took place in a London that still contained "non-places": degenerate wasteland, run-down parts of the city, areas abandoned by the spirit of the times, where the demolition ball had raged without pressure from investors to fill the gaps between the teeth of the city's grin at once with new buildings. "Our architecture is so banal and destructive to the human spirit that walking to work is in itself a depressing experience," wrote Bob Geldof, the singer of the Boomtown Rats. "The streets are shabby and tawdry and litter-strewn, and the concrete is rain-streaked and graffiti-strewn, and the stairwells of the social-engineering experiments are lined in shit and junkies and graffiti."[10] In these places, which had been abandoned by history, the present and the future – blank screens in the postcard genre image that tried to represent the city to the outside world – Punk nestled in as idea and practice. As Jon Savage details in his contribution to this catalogue, there is a close connection between specific London places and a certain sound, a typical "look" and an unmistakeable performative attitude, all of which grew from it. Clubs and squatting houses were artistic paradises in urban hells, where one was happy to spend one or two seasons. What McLaren, Westwood and Reid created in the anonymous bay of 430 King's Road would today be called corporate identity. A novel combination of lines of tradition from aesthetics and the history of ideas, awareness of the present and prognosis of the future, even if these very often – "No Future!" – consisted merely of the negation of possible perspectives. Within this system of consistent parameters, however, there was enormous flexibility: major actors appeared in a wide variety of roles on various plateaus of perceptibility. For example, Jordan, born as Pamela Rooke, was originally known as a confrontational sex-shop saleswoman wearing a fear-inspiring dominatrix outfit and make-up influenced by Mondrian. Later, she appeared in the film *Jubilee*

by Derek Jarman as the post-apocalyptic historian Amyl Nitrate and, dancing the pogo, created the syntax of a feminine body choreography. Linder from Manchester made a name for herself as a singer the band Ludus and also designed record covers for the Buzzcocks their *Spin off* Magazine. Coarse collages where kitchen utensils like toasters and teapots or food items enter into bizarre visual misalliances with naked female bodies: pornography with bondage associations comes in touch with de-sexualised housewife worlds, female identities are presented as constructions constantly threatened by decay, arising from a male attribution logic. The tear-line that comes from assembling newspaper tear-outs and image fragments turns into a suture, the existential seam that combines things that don't go together and this disparity is shown as a wound, a stigma, a deficiency. In the context of *No One is Innocent* Linder is the most striking example of an artist whose works were originally milieu-bound products of the art system and were then, after the implosion of Punk, seamlessly consumed by the gallery and museum industry. A gesture of denial, due to the element of suddenness and flash-like epiphany, became the material from which it was possible to distil a traditional artist career: *Another Music In A Different Kitchen*.

The artist group COUM Transmissions, later transformed into the industrial rock band Throbbing Gristle, can be described as a borderline phenomenon in the meaning of the fluid signifiers of Punk. And this is partly due to their crossing aesthetic, stylistic and gender borders[11] and partly to the attempt to catapult themselves and their public into extreme psychological conditions. Genesis P-Orridge, the chief ideologist, or, if you like, the ideology-destroyer of the collective saw himself more as the author of manifestos and the generator of ideas than as a straight artist. What came about as sounds, images, collages of materials

10   Bob Geldof, quoted from Marcus 1992, p. 13.

11   Genesis P. Orridge, singer and mastermind of Throbbing Gristle and its later incarnation Psychic TV started a "work series" a few years ago, whose purpose was the step-by-step reconstruction of his biological person into a woman; in parallel to that his – now deceased – partner Jackie Breyer had herself changed into a man. The change of sex with hormones, gold crowns, implants and surgical operations, which was also staged as an art exhibition under the title *Painful but Fabulous*, aimed at a "Dematerialization of Identity", blurring the gender boundaries with the help of medical technology, exposing gender allocations as social constructs and the opportunity to break out of the prison of the body and achieve a state of pandrogyny (= multi-gender identity).

and abject gestures in connection with COUM/ Throbbing Gristle did not follow a developmental aesthetic inherent in the material but was the translation of ideas. "We must find methods," P-Orridge wrote, "to break through assumptions, possibilities to take our leave of what is accepted and give up expectations, which are parts of our constructed patterns of behaviour that identify us and can so easily be controlled."[12] Although this ensemble was active long before Punk and was definitely acting with awareness of the material actions, for example, of Viennese Actionism, the maxim that "the future belongs to non-musicians" (P-Orridge) can easily be blended with the dilettante ethos of the kind persistently represented by Mark Perry, the editor of the fanzine *Sniffin' Glue*. COUM/ Throbbing Gristle led to Punk on a parallel track at the same sunset which was to leave the world as a cold star without light or hope, where people would wander around like *Zyklon B Zombies*. P-Orridge, Cosey Fanni Tutti and Co used broken violins, prepared pianos, tape loops and primitive synthesisers to create "psychic detonations" in the heads of the audience. Catharsis through noise, intemperance and excess as a counter-programme to the control society, which Throbbing Gristle had called "wreckers of civilization." During the COUM incarnation of the aesthetic demolition ensemble, P-Orridge put chicken-heads on his penis, and then masturbated. Other props of the Theatre of Cruelty were used tampons, maggots, rotten eggs, feathers and syringes filled with milk, blood and urine, which were used in various series of experiments. It was a kind of "Shock and Awe" tactic with similar media echo-effects to those of McLaren's post-situationist guerrilla concepts, but more indebted to an art-immanent aesthetic of boundary dissolution. Although the assertion of a zero hour or a "blank canvas" in the hot phase of Punk in 1976–77, cutting off all lines to the earlier times of art avant-gardes and music traditions, was always just a myth,[13] there was a feeling of radical change, which, on the far side of the widely publicised

media scandals, manifested itself rather as a subliminal change in preferred materials, expressive codes and colour values. "We destroy in order to create things," Malcolm McLaren claimed. And this destruction applied in particular to style forms and good taste. "Punk [...] embraced everything that cultured people, and hippies, detested," wrote Jon Savage, "plastic, junk food, B-movies, advertising – making money. You got so sick of people being so nice, mouthing an enforced attitude of goodness and health. Punk was liberating and new: the idea of smoking sixty cigarettes a day and staying up all night on speed."[14]

This anti-art attitude, characterised by the singer and theoretician Green Gartside as "messthetics," also worked back on the establishment: artists who already had long careers behind them were allured by the black energy of Punk and let the components of their aesthetics be thrown into confusion by the centrifugal forces that spun from the epicentre of negation into the public arena.

Bill Woodrow, born in 1948, already had a significant solo show in the Whitechapel Art Gallery in 1972. Even in his early works, this sculptor from the generation of Richard Deacon and Tony Cragg used found pieces from rubbish tips, scrap yards and car cemeteries. After a long pause in his work, in 1978, in visual contact with Punk, he enriched his materials with consumer goods such as refrigerators and cars, leftovers from a consumer society charged with history and violence, re-texted into an act of bricolage: a damaged car door against the wall, an armchair with a rifle leaning on it with a formal confusion of metal and wood cut-outs on the other side, as if it were a shotgun painting by William S. Burroughs. Fragments of a language of destruction and anarchy, encoding and recoding totemic messages, translating the immaterial into the concreteness of objects.

In the case of Stephen Willats, born in 1943, the artistic biography goes back even further. He was part of the first generation of British Conceptualists, who set themselves up in critical opposition to traditional, object-related ideas of art. His work materials included questionnaires, Super-8 film cameras and tape recorders, which he used

12 Genesis P-Orridge, in: Simon Reynolds, *Rip it up and start again*, Höfen 2007, p. 240.

13 Punk made use of all possible aesthetics in a kind of ruthless eclecticism: from collage art of the twenties through the emblematicism of Russian Constructivism to neoexpressionist gestures and Art Brut forms of expression.

14 Jon Savage, *England's Dreaming. Sex Pistols and Punk Rock*, London 1991, p. 133.

to document certain social environments before problematising them and making them interpretable in their symbolic complexity. Inspired by the energy of contradiction in Punk, around 1980 Willats focused his interests on the new youth protest cultures and the club scene: his work *Model Dwellings* is named for an electronics club that offered its actors, in proto-futuristic manner, a drop-out scenario from the alienated/alienating present towards the future. Science Fiction and staccato electro-beats, robot-like dance movements and expressionistic make-up. Working together with the members of Model Dwellings, Stephen Willats researched the undergrowth of collective desire. From this came two panes where photos and blocks of text are combined into subjective micro-narratives and puzzle diagrams. With methods of statistics and documentation, the attempt is made, though condemned to failure from its conception, to decipher the culture of desire, based on irrationality, using rational means; in the gap between the goals and the visible result there is a sediment of wishes and fantasies that flourish only in the drop shadow of existence.

Beginning with the primal scream "Anarchy in the UK," the London scene spread in concentric circles until even the established systems found themselves in the wind-tunnel of change. "Anti-art was the start," screamed Poly Styrene of X-Ray Spex with her one-note voice, thus defining the leitmotif for the coming years. And many ran out from the safe harbour of the product society onto the new and exciting spreading sea of possibilities, only to lay to in the first brisk breeze or to capsize in the troubled ocean. For the blink of an eye, Punk was able to become the sound and image language of people discovering their own strength. But this drive was soon exhausted in the act of self-empowerment and what followed developed conventionally on the timeline created by big business. The path from the Sex Pistols to Duran Duran was, in any case, not a great step for mankind. It is a matter of "making slogans without betraying ideas," Walter Benjamin once wrote. But at some point all that remained were slogans, while the ideas had long evaporated. "No Future" became "Too much Future."

New York

I'm painting, I'm painting again
I'm painting, I'm painting again
I'm cleaning, I'm cleaning again
I'm cleaning, I'm cleaning my brain

Talking Heads, *Artists Only*

No New York, 1978

Lydia Lunch was the archetype of the "snotty" teenager from the provinces: born in Rochester and soon bored to death, she moved to New York City at the age of sixteen – without plans but filled with the urge to do something. That could well have ended in the Bowery or in Chelsea Hotel with a needle in her arm. But Lydia, with her band Teenage Jesus and the Jerks, made it onto the sampler *No New York*, which presented only four band from a wealth of possible groups and was produced by Brian Eno. The former glam rock idol and current ambient pioneer more or less gave the next generation a bouquet with the flowers of evil who were now to experience their time of flowering in the capital city of existential border-line existences. What Teenage Jesus produced in the brief time of its existence was, perhaps, the most radical imaginable reduction of rock as an art form: a rhythm alternating between merci-less staccato and infantile hammering, a foul-mouthed screeching slide-guitar and over all that the insistent siren call of Lydia Lunch's voice, who didn't even make an effort to find anything like a melody. That was a kind of music that was thrown out at the people in 15-minute packages, constantly crying "Red Alert" – in the video for the song *Orphans* appropriately visualising thrown bombs, crashing trains and exploding cars.[15] This alarming noise was called "No Wave" – neither a wave nor a fashion nor a compromise in sight. A portrait of the artists as angry young women and men and at the same time a film still from a B-grade movie, combining the noir component with the everyday bohemian misery of existences

without money or a future.[16] In the seventies the Lower East Side was a catastrophe zone forgotten by God and the government: burnt-out houses, building sites towering with garbage, and on every corner down-and-outs drinking from their bottles wrapped in paper bags. At this time New York looked like a cadaver, said the artist Dan Graham in an interview. "The Nixon administration was interested in the souls of the majority, meaning the people outside the big cities, in the suburbs and rural regions. The idea was to cut money to the cities and thus to break them down. Cities fell apart and found themselves in a state of decay."[17] In this urban war zone, where rents were close to zero, all the misfits from the uncool parts of the city, Bronx, Queens and Brooklyn, and outsid-ers with behaviour problems from provincial sites settled in. Inside a geographic space of ten blocks the micro-art scene flourished which – at first – was not interested in money and fame but in self expression, transgression and fluctuating identity constructs involving race, class and gender. "I moved to New York City, as a young artist," said Robert Longo, "for the NYC art world but quickly realized that it was a dying animal. The white walls of the art galleries were rapidly replaced by the dark spaces of art house cinemas and rock clubs. This was where thing were happening. The Punk and No Wave scene was the most stimulating thing happening in NYC at that time – responding to a sense of the failure in the hippie generation and against Presiden Reagan. America was revert-ing to the dark ages."[18] Longo, born in 1953, who was a typical repre-sentative of the first generation to be socialised by the media, with his interest in films, TV, magazines and comics, and projected this fascination into

15 The art of infantile regression was only a transition stage in the aesthetic development of Lydia Lunch. With the record *Queen of Siam* she re-invented herself as a jazz-influenced diseuse and later she shifted her interest to spoken-word performances with sparse musical accompaniment. As the main actor in some films by Richard Kern she was also one of the most striking ap-pearances in New Cinema, which emerged from the surroundings of No Wave and offered performance opportunities to many musicians and personalities of the scene: the New Cinema films, lo-fi und low budget, were made breathtak-ingly fast – in some cases there was no more than a week from writing the script and filming it to the opening night. The film-makers of New Cinema broke with the dominant abstract aesthetics of avant-garde cinema in the style of Stan Brakhage and privileged narratives, reminding one rather of the Un-derground of the early sixties, Warhol and Jack Smith, as well as the B-grade movies of the fifties, filled with trashy stories and extremely brutal tension. No Wave and New Cinema shared a mixture of fascination and envious admiration for all representatives of anti-social or pathological behaviour: murderers, ter-rorists or sect leaders like Jim Jones … James Chance brought this attitude to a climax when he declared to Sounds: "I can't stand liberals. They are so dumb and wishy-washy and their philosophy is so stupid. They are not extreme and I like extreme people." Reynolds 2007, p. 91.

16 The more narrowly defined No Wave scene includes particularly the bands of Brian Eno-Sampler, who achieved a kind of early canonisation: alongside Teenage Jesus also Mars, D.N:A. with Arto Lindsay and James Chance and the Contortions. A broader definition of the term, which is less a musical defini-tion than a confession of a brachial avant-garde attitude, also let groups like Bush Tetras, Material, Swans, the early Sonic Youth, Ut and the Theoretical Girls of Glenn Branca sail under the No Wave banner. In recent years No Wave has been rediscovered on a big scale as a blueprint for contemporary musical aesthetics. There have been many re-publications of old records and excava-tions that have brought to light bands that were even unknown at the time of their existence: Boris Policeband, Pulsallama, Glorious Strangers, Y Pants.

17 Interview with Dan Graham, in: Ulrike Groos, Markus Müller (Hg.), *Make it Funky – Jahresring 45*, *Jahrbuch für moderne Kunst*, Cologne 1998, p. 141.

18 *New York Noise – Art and Music from the New York Underground 1978 – 1988*, London 2007, p. 3.

the urban jungle of the Lower East Side, became, quite consistently, the guitarist of the band Menthol Wars and also played with more conceptually oriented musicians such as Rhys Chatham. In his art he processed the existential confusion of an epoch where, according to the rock critic Dave Marsh, "the economy shrank rather than grew and the innocence of the sixties had been transformed into the cynicism of the seventies" especially in the series *Men in the Cities*: large-format drawings where men – and paradoxically sometimes a woman as well – can be seen in well-cut business suits and twist their bodies into absurd tableaux vivants, their faces distorted with pain. It is as if they are shattered by inner convulsions which are displaced into physical gesture as a paranoid body language.[19] Wall Street was only a couple of stone-throws away and the type of the ruthless broker – pleasure without regrets was a much-quoted slogan from the late seventies – could be studied every day on the streets that bound the decorative misery of Bohemia with the fast money from the stock exchange, as if with an umbilical cord. One part of the no-budget art that grew out of ruins was interested in marking symbolically the no-mans-land of the economic no-go areas, drawing a kind of psychogeographic map where traces of one's own existence could become visible in the public space, which traces, in their sign-like abstraction narrated of complicated self-discoveries in an anonymous sea of buildings. On the occasion of a great garbage strike in New York in 1979, Christy Rupp positioned a rat, the emblematic creature of the Punk epoch, on house walls, thus transforming a negative symbol into a positive sign of resistant survival energy – turned into metaphor by a living creature with which no commercial interests were associated and which is, therefore, as "unnecessary" as the creative environment of the Lower East Side for the distinction-obsessed upper class of Midtown. Richard Hambleton achieved a certain promi-

nence by marking fictitious crime scenes with chalk: volunteers lay down on the asphalt for the artist, thus providing him with the bodily contours of imaginary murder victims. Even more impressive is the *Shadowman* series: silhouettes of men, often wearing hats and coats, who appear in the half-shadow of abandoned back yards or on brick walls and seedy shop fronts as schematic presences and substrates of an absence. Sketchy figures deeply embedded in the creases of American history and mythology, private detectives on the way to solve a crime that the rest of the population doesn't even know has been committed.[20] The idea of not leaving the records of public space to the powerful and the representatives of commercial interests but rather to claim the individual and simultaneously socialisable "I am somebody" with puzzling ciphers of resistance and erratic metaphors from a vital parallel universe ultimately became, in the shape of the "tags" of hip-hop graffiti culture, a widespread form of expression, vigorously combated by the authorities. Nonetheless, the art market soon jumped onto this train and made gallery stars out of such people as Jean-Michael Basquiat and Keith Haring.

While the touchdown of Punk in Great Britain can be fixed fairly precisely at the end of 1976 with the appearance of the Sex Pistols single *Anarchy In The U.K.*, in New York there was never a moment of ignition, a degré zero, which could have functioned as a watershed between pop-cultural formations hostilely opposed to each other. In the seventies London was basically dominated by a constantly more bombastic rock theatricality, while the working class withdrew to the pub on the corner with cosy pub rock. In this case Punk smashed into the situation like a steel fist, introducing new voices, discourses and idiolects, which briefly silenced the saturated modes of expression of the constantly unchanging world. New York, however, as the cultural lighthouse of an East-Coast awareness of difference, had a long tradition of ill-adjusted, illegitimate jazz and rock avant-gardes, from the legendary Exploding Plastic Inevitable, which combined The Velvet

19 It seems that these apparently serious citizens, who let their extremities tremble like puppets or epileptics, were a widespread metaphor of the epoch: the No Wave group of the saxophonist and James Brown impersonator James Chance called itself The Contortions, and the most penetrating scene in Jim Jarmusch's first film, *Permanent Vacation*, shows the sixteen-year-old Allie Parker, a typical lost soul from the provinces with a preference for the forties and fifties, in an ecstatic modern dance, which looks as if a be-bop saxophone solo has been translated into body choreography.

20 Even today, in TV discussion groups, one can discover references to the Shadowman: "Ah, I remember the Shadowman! Reminds me of when I first started hanging out downtown, seeing bands … Always a pleasure. I'm so glad some folks have pix." (www.flickr.com/photos/amolho4/1184509485)

Underground with Andy Warhol, through various minimal variants to the transgender teenage fun of the New York Dolls. Much of this contained elements that were later to become virulent in Punk, but the signs had not yet sorted themselves into a consistent image. And so the Ramones were seen as the first Punk band on the East Coast, even though they came on like an exploded rock group with their long hair plus leather-jacket look. The short, condensed songs, which reminded one of a car chassis where all decorative elements had been removed, and the eagle logo designed by Arturo Vega with its high recognition factor pointed rather in the direction of the nihilist joy in destruction, which also released its testosterone-fed energy in Punk, and was later converted by MTV into the symbolically convertible currency unit Beavis and Butthead: "Beat on the Brat with a Baseball Bat."

Even Patti Smith is assigned to the cultural surroundings of Punk, even though she, according to Jon Savage, moved into a room in the Chelsea Hotel with the young photographer Robert Mapplethorpe as early as 1968, so that she could study the odour of decay in the garden of lust at a central metaphorical place.[21] In the following years the large series of portraits evolved from which ultimately the cover for the first Patti Smith long-playing record, *Horses*, was distilled: an image that, with its androgynous coolness was to become the model for disturbed young people with burning souls and literary ambitions. Patti Smith posed in a white man's shirt with braces and a jacket careless thrown over her shoulder. With her artfully disarranged boy's haircut she looks a little like the photos of Arthur Rimbaud. This similarity is not by chance and probably desired. For the black Romanticism of the dying 19th century definitely left traces in New York Bohemia.[22]

David Wojnarowicz who worked as a photographer, author, painter, film maker and performance artist, had the need, in an act of aesthetic over-identification, to cover over the urban geography where he moved about with the face of a poète

maudit melting into a papier-maché mask. His series of 44 works, *Arthur Rimbaud in New York* shows a young man whose face is replaced with a portrait of Rimbaud held in front of it: a sad clown in an apartment smeared with graffiti, a flâneur in dark, lively streets or a biker posing on his motor-cycle. I is another and yet always the same. The series is said "to have arisen from a particular state of mind that only I know, because I have always felt alien and alienated in this country," wrote Wojnarowicz in his diaries, "I felt like a watcher of my own life while it was played out."[23] The "concert of hells" that Rimbaud conducted, the demons he wanted to sell himself to, the blood he wanted to wade in, the sacred images he wanted to tear down and his recognition that "Life is somewhere else" blended well with a poetry of waste and a politics of excess, which Simon Reynolds wrote about: "The inner city of NY before Aids and Reagan seemed to be wrapped in a bubble of decadence. Drugs, alcohol, polymorphous-perverse sex. The city as a whole may have been on the brink of bankruptcy, but the artists on Lower East Side found opportunities to have a wild time during the collapse."[24]

The tendency to ennoble junky misery and daily rock 'n' roll suicide by have recourse to sleeping stars and Ophelias drifting in the black river, led, however, not uncommonly to pseudo gothic kitsch, which even leading figures like Patti Smith and Richard Hell yielded to. In contrast to the negationism purged of all feeling on the London scene, in New York there was always a tendency to the formulation of pathos, which betrayed its real intentions to an emotional surrogate – and thus had social functions like those of Hollywood melodrama in the fifties, though not for the silent majority but rather for disoriented minorities. On the other hand, the Big Apple was more multi-layered in the complex interplay of art forms than the London Punk scene, which was largely fixated on fashion, design and Top of the Pops. "The boundaries between the disciplines were permeable, and that was very inspiring," said David Byrne of the Talking Heads. "Often there were collabora-

21 Cf. Savage 1991, p. 91.

22 But not only there. The list of Rimbaud stigmata is long and illustrious: Allen Ginsberg, Bob Dylan and Jim Morrison are just the most notable figures from the history of pop and underground literature who felt the "mauvais sang" pulsing through their arteries.

23 David Wojnarowicz, *Close to the Knives: A Memoir of Disintegration*, New York 1991.

24 Reynolds 2007, p. 86.

tions between artists, musicians, film makers and writers. But otherwise, too, everyone knew what was going on outside his or her own field of activity, and that was a very healthy situation. However, it also demanded its fee – one only needs to look at the small number of artists who survived and were able to lead a creative life. There were only a handful, no more than that."[25]

As a blueprint for an aesthetics of transgression and border-crossing, New York had the Warhol factory of the sixties, where creative people, drug addicts, transsexuals and simply hangers-on were constantly re-arranging themselves into new forms of a social sculpture. There was always a connection with art, even if it was often articulated as a rejection of the art system and preferred off spaces, lofts or no-budget micro-galleries to the established gallery scene.[26] The phenomenon that was, as Punk or No Wave, to organise itself a few years later into a big narrative of contradiction and productive wastefulness while simultaneously focusing its gaze consequently had few contact neuroses, when it was a matter of making deviant gestures and consensus-breaching actions of established artists for one's own artistic position. Let's pick out two works here, which had a direct influence on the emerging Punk environment, even though they were created by artists in a completely different context: in the installation *Seedbed* by Vito Acconci, the artist hid himself under a ramp in the Sonnabend Gallery in 1972 and masturbated while he projected his erotic fantasies into the room over him. Even longer-lasting, because it threw the rules and codes of the counter-cultural intelligentsia and advanced academic discourse into confusion, was the reception of an "advertisement" placed by Lynda Benglis in the leading American discourse journal Artforum in 1974. It consisted of a photo showing the artist naked and holding an over-dimensioned dildo in front of her genitals. By using her body as a surface to inscribe various and, in some cases, contradictory signals, Benglis constructed a semiotic labyrinth:

a dark tanned body, apparently glowing with health, where the white traces of the bikini zone can be clearly seen, white Lolita sunglasses, one arm supported on a hip in a challenging manner and, at the same time, a fearfully withdrawn shoulder. Is this self-empowerment or objectivation? Aggressive female search for pleasure or promiscuous behaviour within the terms of the dominant gender economy? Plump imitation of male-coded erotic action or ironic undermining of masculine policy of attribution? The editorial board found the work "extremely vulgar;" Lynda Benglis was making fun "in a shabby way" of the achievements of the women's movement and was exploiting the sensationalism of an uninformed mass audience. But in Punk terminology "exploitation" is anything but a negatively understood concept and, as an alluring, ambivalent puzzle sign in the depths of the public debating arena, in any case better than stringently directed ideologies from left-conservative thinking. And consequently, Lynda Benglis's photo, in its disturbing ambivalence and without losing any frictional heat, was able to wander into the metaphoric cosmos of No Wave. Certain poses of Lydia Lunch as well as the cover of the Contortions' LP *Buy*, have been milked from the same negative dialectics that also left Benglis's self-construction in heroic instability. To us Adorno's words: "It would not take much to see those who are nothing but proof of their own quick life and boastful strength as prepared corpses, who have not been told the news that they have not quite managed to die, for the sake of demographic courtesy."[27]

---

25 *New York Noise*, 2007, p. 1.

26 The singer Alan Vega of the minimal-noise combo Suicide was even a qualified visual artist before he discovered a new outlet for his expressive needs in the rock scene: he produced light sculptures from trashy Catholic figures of saints, plastic toys, pornographic and prominence postcards, which looked like altars of trash culture from a post-apocalyptic America in the near future.

27 Theodor W. Adorno, *Minima Moralia*, Frankfurt a. M. 1998, p. 66.

EINSTÜRZENDE NEUBAUTEN

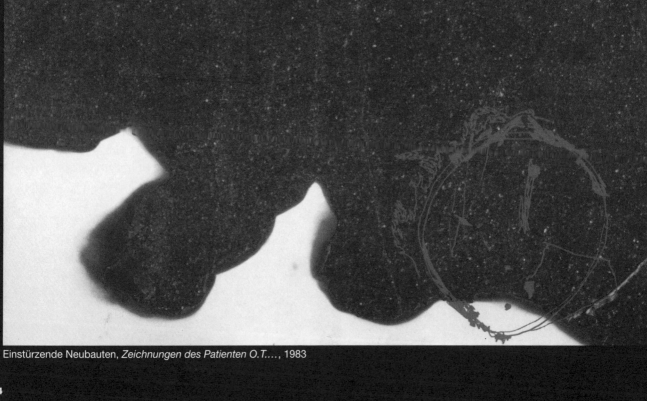

Einstürzende Neubauten, *Zeichnungen des Patienten O.T....*, 1983

Berlin: The possibility of an island. Funded by the West as an outpost of the "Free World," surrounded by East German publicly owned enterprises, the National People's Army, the East German rock band Puhdy, and the endless word-flow of Erich Honecker: "Vorwärts immer, rückwärts nimmer!" (Forwards forever, backwards never!) the island of Berlin, isolated by the "antifascist wall of protection," which created identities on both sides of the political field of action. "I found the wall really great", said Annette Humpe, the Berlin myth emerging in the late seventies turning hit-parade cash with the band Ideal. "Berlin was so beautifully surrounded. That protected us from the stupid West Germans."[28] Rents were low, closing times liberal, the mood bad, the search for pleasure gigantic. And in this way Berlin became the test station for the end of the world, where you gazed into the abyss so long that it started to stare back at you. Around the pubs and bars in Schöneberg and Kreuzberg, such as Risiko, Mitropa, SO 36, Zest, Milchbar, Swing, etc., an environment grew up with neo-existentialists dressed in black, who stimulated a condition of long-term mobility according to the motto "Bring your body to the party" and strove for an inner convulsion stimulated by pills. The city became the space for possibilities on the far side of imposed routes, systematic thinking processes and enforced business models. If you read a statement of Jürgen Teipel, the musician and DJ fetish of the time, in his oral history *Verschwende deine Jugend* (Waste Your Youth), you could almost believe that Guy Debord had written the script for such urban expeditions: "When we went down the Ku'damm, we didn't just go down the Ku'damm. We had our own geography. We walked through Berlin as if we were going through the jungle. That was our own parallel Berlin. We didn't even see most of the people and most of the things. Blacked them out. Simply surfed through. We painted our own map of how Berlin looks. The collection points we have, the routes we go and the deviations we take."[29] It's no wonder that at this time David Bowie and Iggy Pop, with their fine feeling for movements of aesthetic difference and paradigmatic reshufflings,

settled in the city. In particular, David Bowie's LP *Low*, with its subliminal traces of limp excesses and impenetrable secret operations, gave witness to a morbid fascination with the echo effects of a fin-de-siècle decadence that was current in the half-shadows of war ruins. The title implied a final question: *How low can you go*? For strategic life on the margins or even outside the norms of civilisation belonged to the noblest duties of those players of the game without borders which was on in Berlin from midnight to midnight. Reports of the time tell of consciously staged rituals of disgust aiming to test the psychological limits of one's own organism. Blixa Bargeld, the singer and dark prince of Einstürzenden Neubauten, lived in a basement where, for the sake of simplicity, one urinated into a yoghurt cup at the side of the bed. And in the Boutique Eisengrau of Gudrun Gut and Bettina Köster, who were musically active in the groups Mania D and later Malaria!, a group of aesthetic extreme sportspeople decorated the display windows with remnants of food. "It looked very good. Bread rolls and sliced cheese," said Alex Hacke from the Einstürzenden Neubauten. "That was this big recycling number that Punk was supposed to be originally. Our haircuts as well. Rat cuts. Simply holes cut in. That was harder than the normal Punk Rock number. It was a high point of ugliness. For me that was, in fact, the main thing: debating with dirt."[30]

Punk had arrived in Germany, as in the rest of the continent, with a delay of two or three years. At that time people in England were already talking about Post-Punk and the musical field was opening up to experimental sounds (Pop Group, This Heat, early Human League), while style features, reduced to a few surrogate points, were conquering the boutiques and hairdressing salons. For that reason the scene in Berlin split into two camps once the signals had been received. They were not only indifferent to each other but sometimes faced each other as enemies: a three-chord Punk in the tradition of the Pistols and later Prol-Punk bands like Sham 69 combined

28 Jürgen Teipel, *Verschwende deine Jugend*, Frankfurt a. M. 2001, p. 115.
29 Teipel 2001, p. 110.

30 Teipel 2001, p. 237.

with two-thought political slogans,[31] as well as an (anti-)art milieu, where Punk was seen as a break in the weave of the always-the-same and worked at its own version of "après moi le déluge" in close spiritual proximity to *No New York*. There were interfaces where these two scenes met each other. One was Club SO 36, which was managed for a short time by Martin Kippenberger (and Andreas Rohe) and was designed as a non-place and free-space open to all sides. Here there were innumerable gigs with traditional and avant-garde Punk ensembles, here no-budget film scenes from what was later known as *Berlin Super 80* with directors like the early Jörg Buttgereit, Martin Jelinski, Christoph Doering and Maye & Rend-schmidt were performed,[32] here the Neue Wilde painters – Helmut Middendorf, Rainer Fetting, Salomé, Elvira Bach – came together from Moritz-platz and elsewhere. The inner tension that gave the project a precarious status from the beginning may have been an enlivening element for a while.[33] But at some point the unresolved contradictions between the particular interests came to a rapid, inglorious end: Punks from the "we don't want no poli-pigs" fraction raided the Club on 11 November 1979, aiming to "socialise" the till, because, in their opinion, the entrance prices were too high. Kippenberger finally gave up his ambitions of mediating between art and Punk, on the model of Carmen Knoebel in the Düsseldorf Ratinger Hof, and left the field to other players.

But the avant-garde scene itself was also split: on one wing, which wanted to assure itself of the authenticity of its being-in-the-world by catapult-ing its own subjectivity – or what they thought was that – into physical and psychological extreme states[34] (Einstürzende Neubauten, etc.) and, on the other wing, a sceptical-ironic fraction. The latter did not believe that a presumptive uniqueness was to be found as the core of the existential, but was interested in gaining a perspective on the world by the deconstruction of the absence of uniqueness (Die Tödliche Doris, endart, etc.). In the course of time the Neubauten became synonymous with a certain form of the Berlin underground milieu, so that it is difficult today to tie up the subtle movements of difference and aesthetic disparities in comparison with other players. That has something to do with the sheer long life of the band, which is still active today, but also with the repressive mass of its world of symbols, which claims interpretational hegemony over an entire subcultural epoch. Einstürzende Neubauten were the ideal model of an apocalyptic crash-and-bang ensemble and Blixa Bargeld was the catalyst, able to translate their "Bring the Noise!" into fluctuations of the soul and jagged scraps of language. The myth of the band is due largely to a tough but just materiality, which has now long been lost overboard but which at that time was read as remorseless consistency: percussion instruments from scrap metal and everyday objects,[35] performances at the boundary of bodily capacity, not rarely ending in self-mutilation, infernal screams teleporting existential pain and solipsistic absence of mind through the rawness of the voice: the artist as exemplary sufferer, a soul forgotten on cold stare in the whirl of contingencies. What seemed convincing back then as a radical manifestation between noise and an uneasy scratching and scraping sacrificed some of its suggestiveness under change contextual conditions: now one heard rather the false tones in the sound of chaos, hollow pathos in the stilted linguistic images. The Einstürzende Neubauten enjoyed playing the role

31 The groups called themselves PVC, Ffurs, Katapult, Vitamin A, etc., took very few musical risks and occupied themselves in a rather simple way with the classical themes of rebellious youth: *Linker Spießer* (Aetztussis), *Tanz aus dem Ghetto* (Zerstoerte Jugend), *Kraft durch Bier* (Ceresit).

32 At this time video was still a relatively expensive medium, wrote Ralf S. Wolkenstein in the booklet on *Berlin Super 80*. This is why many young directors still used the already obsolete Super 8 format: "You could get cheap cameras at every flea market. Super 8 was mainly a silent medium. For this reason the directors let their current favourite numbers run on the sound track for their first films. Later there were specially composed soundtracks for certain works. In this way there was some overlapping between the film and music scenes." Ralf S. Wolkenstein, "West Berlin was an Island," in: *Berlin Super 80*, Monitorpop Entertainment 2005.

33 "The SO 36 was in the middle of Kreuzberg. It was a former supermarket, a huge flat room. Totally empty. And there was neon lighting all around. I remember one Berlin avant-garde band that performed there. And for Punks avant garde was undesirable. So they knew what was coming to them and they came on stage wrapped in garbage bags with steel helmets on their heads. Of course they had all the more things thrown at them." Frank Z. of the Hamburg band Abwärts, in: Teipel 2001, pp. 194.

34 *Ich und die Wirklichkeit* (Me and Reality) was the name of a famous piece by the radical minimalist duo DAF: "Me and me in real life. Me and me in reality. Me and me in the real world. Me and me. I feel so strange. Reality is coming. Reality is coming."

35 "Metal had a strange attraction for me. There are some pieces of steel I simply have to have. Especially big and heavy ones. And that's why I looked all the more around building sites and took things for myself, which I redeployed as furniture or music devices: drainpipes, oil tanks and especially ventilation shafts made of metal. They were really beautiful. New metal." Andrew Unruh, drummer of Einstürzende Neubauten, in: Teipel 2001, p. 240.

of spies in the "house of lies," but it is extremely doubtful whether they managed to oppose the persuasive discourse of the appeals to consume with a verbal and acoustic expression of being at one with themselves in a condition of ecstasy. "As a matter of principle, that was pure art of expression," writes Frank Apunkt Schneider in his book *Als die Welt noch unterging* (When the World Was Still Going Under), "the cry of a stale mixture of expressiveness and Existentialism; the pain of the artist's soul and gestalt therapy packed in a more or less new language for the audience – at least that's what it seems to be now … The Neubauten were operating with already slightly obsolescent artistic ideas of classical Modernism: a transference of art into life as lived, depth, soul, pain, genius, Primitivism, obsessiveness … The Neubauten were perhaps the prototype of an intensity band – and real cannons of end-of-the-world feelings."[36]

The banner of intensity had also been pulled on by the Neue Wilde, who helped the epoch find its visual signature. Many of the large formats rocked out with a liberated brush from Berlin painting studios looked like optical transformations of Neubauten texts: "Sag nein, nein nein nein, negativ nein, das Leben ist nicht bunt, geballt gehen wir zugrunde." (Say no, no, no, no, negative no, life is not bright and colourful, we are going down all screwed up together.) Life may not have been bright or colourful, but the paintings were: fleshy red as on the sheets in the work *Fuck 1* by Salomé, where a naked man twists his body wearing a black mask, poisonous yellow in *Rote Liebe*, an orgiastic interweaving of bodies that lets the dynamics of erotic expenditure continue to tremble as a stilled life. After the shock caused by their first intense performance the young Neue Wilde were often accused of conservatism and an unreflected return to traditional, representational painting styles, in particular the Expressionism of the twenties. But this criticism falls short: it was less a matter of founding continuities than of announcing complicity with immediately precedent avant-gardes and their elaborated formats. In their strivings for authenticity the Neue Wilde were certainly comparable with the Neubauten. The con-

crete quality of the figures was set as an antithesis to an abstract art that owed much to the teleological, Hegelian model of history and had triumphed ideologically. But it was not a matter of enrolling with another concept in the tradition of the fine arts, but of developing an eclectic style on the far side of that tradition, which helped itself anywhere that seemed to offer rewards and was responsible only to intuitive self-expression and the nerve impulses of individual interior contemplation: in particular, the Berlin painters had "striven for a postmodern synthesis of modernity and tradition, which actually mistrusted both," wrote Schneider, "and also needs both so that each can keep the other in check. In particular the works of the Berlin fraction showed considerable similarities with the Expressionism of the artist group Die Brücke. But also with the Abstract Expressionism of Jackson Pollock, whose gestural painting manner was transferred to an object-oriented work. Many of the pictures that resulted from this look like a struggle between pre-modern representational and avant-garde abstract traditions."[37]

If one examines the individual careers of several artists who became famous at that time, one gets the impression that the complicated balancing act of styles and approaches could succeed only in a condition of pre-reflexive appropriation and conceptless dissemination. At the moment when it became a fixed, easily recognised and repeatable manner triviality was already peeping around the corner. But what can you do – life goes on, even if the historical moment has long passed. And so, from today's point of view the artistic projects have grown old that prescribed a priori an aesthetic and personal long-term mobility for themselves like endart or, even when they started, an expiry date, like Die Tödliche Doris (1980–1987). endart saw itself as a contextual group that set deterritorialised activities going buried in the depths of a specific social and cultural milieu, tried out attitudes and then rejected them again: "BERLIN-KREUZBERG. Demolition and restoration quarter, Eldorado of extreme subculture," wrote Wolfgang Max Faust in an account of the work and (anti-)ideology of the group. "A CONTEXT can be recognised that takes up and helps to form the experience of the surroundings: a centre for Turkish guest workers and their families, the neighbourhood of pensioners, workers and Punks. This quarter of West Berlins is dominated by extremes: dull survival blends with revolutionary joy in existence, new secondhand elegance strikes alcoholic indifference, Bhagwan sects compete with street gangs and banal existence ... endart was/is part of this life context."[38]

Art as streaming, flowing, permanent exchange, constructive dialectics of a with-one-another/against-one-another, which sometimes dies away in the cacophony of continuous communication and then, on the other hand, produces tangible objects: Kindergarten provocation, but without an ideological stamp – the swastika! the erect penis! – Art Brut as a method to squeeze perfectly normal madness back into the beer bottle it has just escaped from, plasticene men (and women), art from the ontological cosy corners where people give birth to hedgehogs and policemen are snapped French-kissing in the zoo. Mens sana and yet bent three times around the corner of rational world perception. "Not the statics of individual works but a total association is sought, which reaches beyond the group."[39]

At the beginning of the "Berlin disease" Tödliche Doris was an important interface of (dis)organisation and ideological (de)construction: Wolfgang Müller, Nikolaus Utermöhlen plus varying female players were mainly responsible for initiating the *Die große Untergangsshow* (Big Decline Show), staged by the "dilettante geniuses" from Berlin in all their aesthetic and philosophical incompatibility: Einstürzende Neubauten, DIN A Testbild, Frieder Butzmann, Sprung aus den Wolken, Leben und Arbeiten and so forth. The event may have been fleeting, but the concept remained persistent for a long time: *Geniale Dilletanten* (Dilettante Geniuses) was also the name of a collected volume edited by Wolfgang Müller for Merve-Verlag, which could be read as a kind of manifest of a scene which refused to respond to the appeals of established culture and politics, which sometimes – see the steel drums of the Neubauten – made its own instruments and ig-

nored the distinction between high art and low art – at that time still an heroic project. Dilettantism – with in-built typing errors – meant an attitude of strategically refusing technology and craftsmanship, in order to reach an in-between position while circling around rituals of aesthetic discipline: a psychogeographical (N)owhere, mentally liberated territories, heterotopic zones in the meaning of Foucault: "to an extent, places outside all places, even though they can be placed."[40]

Even before the term "Geniale Dilletanten" became a label thought-lazy journalists could use to classify noise-sounds, deviant forms of behaviour and unorthodox orders of clothing – Blixa Bargeld's famous gumboots! – Die Tödliche Doris had already departed: "It was a matter of constantly inquiring into one's own identity again and again," said Wolfgang Müller in an interview: "and of positioning the fine cut of one's outer appearance as the central theme of the work of art. Whenever the Tödliche Doris tried to make even a slight attempt at a definition it reacted by striving for further alternatives."[41]

Instead of frozen poses, images and artistic actions, therefore, fluidity, changes to aggregate conditions, exploding saturated production strategies. Originally started as a kind of rock band, the Tödliche Doris quickly perfected itself as a subversion diva simultaneously dancing on a thousand plateaus, like a striptease dancer letting its aesthetic wrappings fall one by one, only to reveal under them more materialisations of art weave and philosophical-theoretical sailors' yarn. In addition to many normal LPs and tapes, they also brought out an invisible record, which could be heard only if you played the albums *Unser Debüt* and *Sechs* at the same time on two record players. The engaged the commercial Gerry Belz Show Combo, who presented their normal dance repertoire, and mixed the sound with noises. With an infant wearing a swastika T-shirt in the main role, they made the Super-8-film *Das Leben des Sid Vicious* (The Life of Sid Vicious). There were also: grotesque blow-ups of autograph cards or,

38   endart – *Flucht aus dem Dschungel des Lasters*, Berlin 1994, p. 13.

39   Faust 1994, p. 14.

40   Michel Foucault, "Andere Räume" (1967), in: Karlheinz Barck (Ed.), *Aisthesis: Wahrnehmung heute oder Perspektiven einer anderen Ästhetik*, Leipzig: Reclam, 1993, p. 39.

41   "Ingenious Dilettantes?" – Interview with Wolfgang Müller, in: *Berlin Super 80*, Monitorpop Entertainment 2005.

in *Material für die Nachkriegszeit* (Material for the Postwar Period), a puzzle made of hundreds of discarded or torn slot-machine passport photos. Every conceptual gesture is only suggested, every step on the long march through the infiltrations performed as a tap and grope trial without guarantee of artistic dignity and a place in the "Hall of Fame" of rebellious "bad-ass" attitudes.

In this sense, the Tödliche Doris, although as unpunky as can be imagined, perhaps transformed the original impulse of this antagonistic non-movement most radically into an aesthetic of universal scepticism. Instead of the subject escaping from all limitations, in the Tödliche Doris the fury of disappearance and the masks of desire dominate events – a desire that cannot be determined even by a Lacan tying a Borromean knot. New singers on the songlines that point to infinity and let a voice be heard that is still producing echoes in 2008 even though it was raised in 1976: "For a time, as if by magic – the pop magic in which the connection of certain social facts with certain sounds creates irresistible symbols of the transformation of social reality – that voice worked as a new kind of new free speech."[42]

42 Marcus 2003, p. 2.

LONDON

Jamie Reid, Sex Pistols, *God Save The Queen*, 1976

**god save the queen
the fascist regime
they made you a moron
potential h-bomb**

**god save the queen
she ain't no human being
there is no future
in england's dreaming**

God Save The Queen, Sex Pistols

NEVER MIND THE BOLLOCKS

HERE'S THE

Sex PisTOls

Jamie Reid, Sex Pistols, *Never Mind The Bollocks Here's The Sex*

Jamie Reid, Sex Pistols, *Holidays In The Sun*, 1977

Jamie Reid, Sex Pistols, *Anarchy In The U.K.*, 1976

The Clash, *The Clash*, 1977

white riot – i wanna riot
white riot – a riot of my own
black people gotta lot a problems
but they don't mind throwing a brick
white people go to school
where they teach you how to be thick
an' everybody's doing
just what they're told to
an' nobody wants
to go to jail!

White Riot, The Clash

Throbbing Gristle, *T.G.*, 1977

X-Ray Spex, *Germfree Adolescents*, 1978

**bind me tie me
chain me to the wall i wanna be a slave
to you all**

**chain-store chain-smoke
i consume you all
chain-gang chain-mail
i don't think at all**

**oh bondage up yours
oh bondage no more**

Oh Bondage, Up Yours!, X-Ray Spex

The World's End: London Punk 1976–1977

Jon Savage

Jon Savage, *Untitled (London)*, 1977

To complete my sensation of dislocation, alienation perhaps, a solitary laser beam hung flickerless over London, like a single wire of an imprisoning mesh. Didn't they feel it too? I asked my friends. Didn't they sense, in the condition of their city that night, symptoms of disintegration? It was like someone who had suffered a breakdown, I said, whose personality is split, splintered or possibly in abeyance.

Jan Morris, "London Intermezzo: The Precarious Rituals of a City Between Performances," *Rolling Stone 263*, April 20, 1978

The wind howls through the empty stones looking for a home
I run through the empty stone because I'm all alone.

Joe Strummer for The Clash, *London's Burning*, 1976

The London within which Punk rock flourished – for two short years: 1976 and 1977 – was a world away from today's global megalopolis. Major cities change very rapidly, of course, but Punk rock happened during a time of turmoil in London's history, a crisis of confidence, of money, and of extremist politics. Of course some areas, like the West End, haven't changed that much: but they were not where the focus was or where the culture was made.

London felt very threatening during the late seventies: violent, under siege and paranoid. When I think of my home city in that period, it's in images of streets and streets of corrugated iron; line upon line of policemen; rows of derelict buildings awaiting demolition; the buddleia blooming in the bomb sites. And in the background, looming like primeval monsters, the tower blocks that would soon become a social realist cliché.

This was caused by very real deprivation. In common with other major cities in America and Europe, London was suffering the effects of a deepening recession that, among other things, had a direct impact on the urban fabric. During the sixties and seventies, whole areas had been emptied or razed in preparation for new builds but, as the money ran out, so was London caught between destruction and regeneration.

The relationship of Punk to urbanism was intense and integral. At its very beginnings, Punk was an international movement, a creative and emotional response to the situation that young dissidents and outcasts found themselves in the mid seventies. The hippies had advocated removing themselves to the country: the very early punks celebrated the dead cities that they would revive through the force of their vision.[1]

The new generation celebrated decay and vacancy. Dereliction offered an opportunity to live cheaply near the city center, in cheap flats and squats. In the empty spaces and blank spaces, the imagination could run riot. The metropolis was no longer seen as the source of all evil, but as a playground that, for the overstimulated and undernourished young, allowed community at the same time as it gave up unexpected illuminations. The city was wide open.

London Punk was zoned by its two major groups, the Sex Pistols (Chelsea and World's End/Soho) and the Clash (North Kensington/Ladbroke Grove). At the same time, Throbbing Gristle (Hackney/ London Fields) offered a complementary and contemporary dissonance. All three drew their energy and their character from their surroundings that, in each case, are barely recognizable today. Maybe

---

1   Many of those involved with Punk remember this time in terms of possibility. The film Director Mary Harron began writing for *Punk Magazine* soon after moving to New York in 1975: "Part of the feeling at that time was this longing for oblivion that you were about to disintegrate, go the way of the city. Yet that was something almost mystically wonderful." David Thomas, the founder member of Pere Ubu, was part of a group of people who moved back into the center of Cleveland, Ohio: "The city I loved was one that everyone else hated, it was totally deserted, people fled when the sun went down. It was run down, but we thought it was beautiful at the time of youth when you're prone to romanticism."

the buildings are the same, but the atmosphere isn't.

An unstable mixture of Mod West London and Irish Finsbury Park, the Sex Pistols were put together in Malcolm McLaren and Vivienne Westwood's shop at 430 King's Road. Now that it has become an international tourist site, it's hard to remember that the World's End once was that: at the very wrong end of Chelsea, a corner too far for the fashion victims.[2] It demanded some commitment, just to get there, because there was nothing else. Once the Sex Pistols got going, McLaren found them a rehearsal room at the back of number 6, Denmark Street – on the edge of Soho. The space was both practical – at various points one or two members of the band lived there – and highly symbolic, in the heart of London's Tin Pan Alley: the area that Laurence Harvey had made his beat in the 1960 film *Expresso Bongo* – a classic British rock film and a major influence on McLaren's relentless hustler persona. Early Sex Pistols' shows oscillated between satellite towns like St. Albans or Welwyn Garden City, outer suburbs like Chislehurst, and central London venues like art schools and, infamously, a Soho strip club called El Paradise. Occasionally, they were forced to use existing venues on the pub rock circuit but they continued to play out of the way places while developing a residency at the 100 Club, on the North side of Oxford Street.

A stalwart of the postwar Trad Revival Jazz scene, this long-standing venue was directly plugged into the Soho underworld – the subculture investigated in Raymond Thorp's *Viper*, the most notorious British drug memoir of the 1950s. In autumn 1976, Malcolm McLaren found an office for the Sex Pistols' management company, Glitterbest, in an old Victorian building (now demolished) called Dryden Chambers, a few hundred yards from the venue. McLaren had long had a fascination with this thoroughfare. In the early seventies he planned a film about the changing patterns of consumerism as reflected the street's chain stores. Oxford Street runs from Marble Arch – close to the site of Tyburn, where public hangings were held until the

late 18th century – and narrows as it goes eastwards towards Holborn: McLaren insisted that this was a piece of crowd control constructed after the 1780 "Gordon Riots."[3]

Down a side street a few hundred yards away from the 100 Club was the lesbian club, Louise's that became an inner circle Punk hangout in the autumn of 1976. There the Sex Pistols, the Clash and the groups that would soon follow them into the spotlight mingled with members of the disaffected, flamboyant suburbanites who would become known as the Bromley Contingent. Oh, and a few "very, very resentful middle-aged, middle class dykes."[4]

The Bromley Contingent – Siouxsie Sioux, Steve Severin, Billy Idol, Berlin and others – all came from London's South East quadrant. Former Bowie and Roxy fans, obsessed with the film *Cabaret*, they were most at home in the gay bars of the period, the Sombrero, the Masquerade, Rob's and Louise's: only there they would not be hassled. As did, in the early days, the Sex Pistols and The Clash: for they were outrageous for the time. This link-up between another outcast subculture has been ill-reckoned in many Punk histories.[5] Although it was nearly a decade since its partial decriminalisation, homosexuality was still misunderstood and demonised – too often forced to live in the shadows. The gay clubs were often situated in forgotten parts of the city, and thus – apart from the freedom of dress and behaviour that they offered – were part of the Punk remapping of London.

The most celebrated example of this was in the way that a former gay bar became the hottest Punk club in London. Chaguaramas was, in Berlin's words, "a dingy dive where the worst transvestites in the world went, and all these businessmen."[6] After the national scandal caused by the Sex Pistols' appearance on television, Punk was shut out of most venues, and this basement club in a decayed part of London was its home for a season.

---

3   A reconstruction of these riots forms the opening scenes of the 1980 film, *The Great Rock 'n' Roll Swindle.*

4   Berlin in interview with Jon Savage for *England's Dreaming.*

5   Which have tended to concentrate on the gang machismo of the boys in the band.

6   Berlin in interview with Jon Savage for *England's Dreaming.*

2   One shop that was right on the main drag was Acme Attractions, run by Don Letts and Jeanette Lee in the Antiquarius building. This later moved a few shops down toward Chelsea Town Hall and become Boy in early 1977. Both were reviled by Vivienne Westwood, as tainted by trendiness.

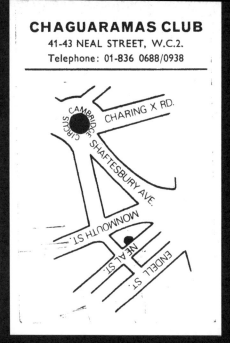

Chaguaramas was sourced by Gene October, the singer of Chelsea, who had contacts in the gay underworld of the time. In 1976, when the Roxy opened, Covent Garden was derelict: the fruit and veg market that had been the area's raison d'être had shut in 1974. Into this interzone poured the punks, their confrontational dress finding its perfect setting: the brick walls and smashed windows that would become an iconic cliché in 1977.

There was another aspect to this dynamic. The Bromley Contingent had a heightened view of the inner London. "I always gravitated towards the city," Siouxsie remembered; "I hated suburbia. Some people stuck to their local town, like Bromley. You could hang out there and feel pretty grown up, but I hated it. I thought it was small and narrow minded."[7] From 1976 on, London became a glamour magnet for a whole generation of young suburbanites.

At the same time, the Sex Pistols' origin in number 430 helped to transform the King's Road. As the name changed from Sex to Seditionaries at the end of 1976, the group became nationally infamous and the shop became a place of pilgrimage. The King's Road strip now stretched for a good mile from Sloane Square in the East to World's End in the West and, as well as Boy, a whole selection of outlets arose to cater to the burgeoning Punk trade.

Many of these were concentrated at the World's End bend: Johnson's and American Classics were

Jon Savage, montage *Strength Health* for *The Secret Public* with Linder, 1977

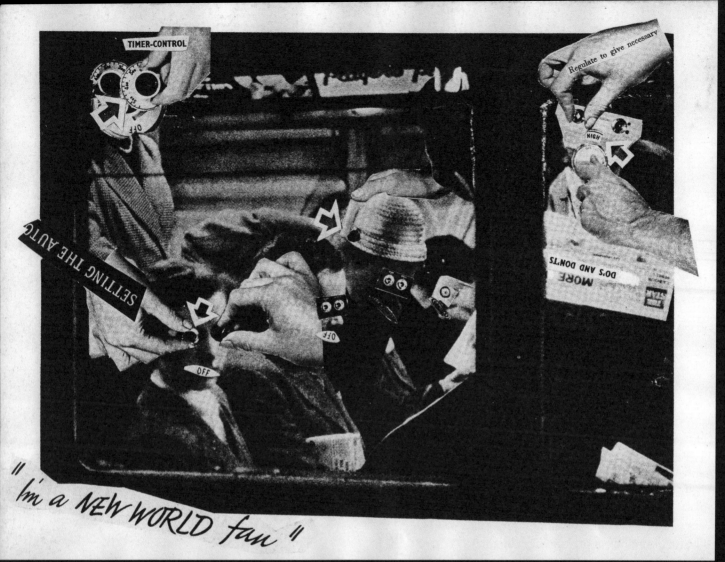

TIMER-CONTROL

SETTING THE AUTO

Regulate to give necessary

MORE DO'S AND DON'TS

"I'm a NEW WORLD fan"

Jon Savage, montage *New World* for *The Secret Public* with Linder, 1977

already there, but in spring 1977 the Beaufort Market opened – with a stall run by Poly Styrene (X-Ray Spex) among others. Just on the other side of the road, Roxy Music designer Antony Price opened his new shop Plaza. From the spring on, hundreds of punks walked the strip, leading up to the massed disturbances of the next eighteen months.

London Punk's second major zone – North Kensington – was marked out by The Clash. Singer Joe Strummer was a veteran of the massed squats in the Chippenham, just north of the Harrow Road near Maida Vale. As he remembered, "someone in the council had decided they were going to knock down about a hundred fine Victorian terrace houses, and it was between deciding and them actually knocking them down that the squat culture flourished."[8]

Many other Punk luminaries squatted during that period, including Johnny Rotten and Sid Vicious (Hampstead) and future members of The Slits, The Clash and Public Image Ltd. (Davis Road, Hammersmith). Clash co-writer Mick Jones squatted in Davis Road, before returning to live in Wilmcote House, one of the huge tower blocks at Harrow Road, just east of Ladbroke Grove. His view from the 19th floor inspired The Clash's *London's Burning*.

In their early days, the Clash were hyper-modernist. Their territory was Ladbroke Grove, Notting Dale and the Harrow Road, all areas marked by dereliction. Through the center of these empty zones ran the Westway, the only motorway to slice through inner London. Influenced by the J.G. Ballard's *Crash* (1973) and *High Rise* (1975) they saw this part of London as a mutant environment that, despite its brutality, offered freedom.

Surrounded by empty spaces – like broken teeth

8   Joe Strummer in interview with Jon Savage for *England's Dreaming*.

in the face of the city – The Clash encoded emptiness into their music. Influenced by the dub reggae that was ever present in London during that period, they introduced the idea of drop-out: sudden gaps in their instrumental attack that highlighted tribal, pounding drums or the barked rants of Joe Strummer. This was, briefly, a science-fiction sound – before a more conventional social realism took over.

The Portobello Road area loomed large in their mythology after the big riot at the August 1976 Notting Hill Carnival. Caught up in what was essentially a black struggle, they felt powerless: the result was their first single, *White Riot*. The disturbances were also featured in the photograph on the back of their first album, released in April 1977: ranks of policeman run with their truncheons as the Westway looms large at the top of the picture.

Ladbroke Grove had long between a West Indian stronghold. As part of their identification with the area's atmosphere, The Clash covered Junior Murvin's *Police and Thieves* on their first album, and hired famed Jamaican producer Lee Perry to work on their summer 1977 single, *Complete Control*. Their fourth single, *White Man in Hammersmith Palais*, described the atmosphere of a reggae show at that famous venue.

The Clash's humanist, multicultural approach would eventually help them to mass success: it arose out of North Kensington, in the same way that the Warholian carnival of early Sex Pistols' shows came out of the suburban/Soho milieu. In the same way, the Sex Pistols' base in Denmark Street gave forewarning of their wish to enter the heart of the music industry – as they did when they signed to EMI Records in October 1976.

For Throbbing Gristle, it was the blasted environment of Hackney – where poverty was not temporary but ingrained – that shaped their monochrome, brutalist dystopias. They were not as far from Punk as might be imagined: they played at the ICA a few weeks after The Clash on the opening night of the infamous COUM Transmissions *Prostitution* show, and their support act was Gene October's Chelsea, renamed LSD just to annoy everyone.

Indeed, the tabloid furore that followed the *Prostitution* show in late November – with COUM cast as the "wreckers of civilisation" – can now be regarded as a dry run for the scandal that occurred in December 1976, when the Sex Pistols swore live on teatime TV. In both cases, it marked the collision of aggressive, avant-garde aesthetics with the beginnings of the powerful right-wing backlash that would eventually result in the Thatcher governments.

In 1976, COUM were best known for Mail Art and Performance Art actions: when they decided to add members and move into music, they took the parallel name Throbbing Gristle. Their principal base was at founder Genesis P-Orridge's house in Beck Road, Hackney – a Victorian street full of decayed working-men's houses, which were largely squatted by artists and bohemians. This felt like a dehumanised, dangerous part of the city. "Throbbing Gristle's studio was," as P-Orridge remembered, "at Martello Street in the basement of a factory, and also next to London Fields Park, which is where a lot of the plague victims were buried. So through the concrete walls of the basement were thousands of dead plague victims, so we nicknamed it the Death Factory, but I always saw the Death Factory as a metaphor for industrial society as well, like *Metropolis*."[9]

Released in 1977, the group's darkly ambient first album reflected this environmental worldview. P-Orridge: "When we'd finished producing the tapes that became *The Second Annual Report*, I remember going outside at Martello Street as a train passed on the railway line, and there was a transistor radio blaring round the corner, and a sawmill cutting up wood, and I just said, we haven't invented anything. We've just put down what's here all the time."[10]

The zenith of London Punk was the Sex Pistols' River Thames boat trip on the Jubilee Bank Holiday, June 1977. To promote the single, *God Save The Queen* – which although banned right across the media was rising fast up the charts – their record company Virgin hired a pleasure boat called *Queen Elizabeth* ostensibly for a German

9   Genesis P-Orridge in interview with Jon Savage for *England's Dreaming*.
10 Genesis P-Orridge in interview with Jon Savage for *England's Dreaming*.

synthesizer group. When the Captain found out that it was for notorious the Sex Pistols, he was not pleased.

As the boat floated up river towards the Houses of Parliament, the Sex Pistols began playing *Anarchy In The U.K.* – an extraordinarily symbolic moment, as the group laid its claim to be the real face of England, not the nauseating nostalgia of the Royal Silver Jubilee. In the press iconography of the time, images of Punk and the Sex Pistols vied with pictures of the Queen and the Royals – both icons of a divided country on the edge of a nervous breakdown.

The lyrics of *God Save The Queen* laid it all out: "god save your mad parade", "there is no future in England's dreaming." For many young Britons, the Queen's Silver Jubilee – she had acceded to the throne 25 years before – was a rotten lie, a return to the early 1950s, just after England had won the war and the old class structure was dominant. In 1977, this dream was manifestly threadbare, and nowhere more than in London's derelict areas. Beneath the stupidity of its media face, Punk was concerned with truth and perception: as Johnny Rotten had sung on *I Wanna Be Me*, "now is the time to realize, to have real eyes." The drama of the Jubilee boat trip – enacted on the river right in front of England's Parliament – brought present realities into collision with state-sponsored fantasies of the past. The cry of "No Future" allowed the future to happen.

In their very different ways, the three keynote London groups of the period worked on the same principle: that the existential truth was to be found, not in the wealthy areas that existed and will always exist in London, but in its forgotten interzones. Not just because they embodied the desperate situation of England at that time, but because they highlighted the fact that the city was porous, that it could be bent to the aesthetic or dissident will.

Within these empty spaces the punks – just like the Lettrists had done a couple of decades before[11] – could remap the city. The energy that they poured into districts and buildings that had been rejected by everyone else offered a kind of instinctive urban regeneration that, twinned with the media concentration on London that occurred in the Jubilee Year of 1977, could now be regarded as the start of the capital's climb back up to its present world city status.

Just as Punk rock, in enshrining failure, made success very difficult for those groups who were, then the consequences of its love for the inner city had the effect of closing down the circumstances in which it flourished. Beginning in the early 1980s, the regeneration of London has been thorough and brutal: there are now almost no empty spaces within the inner city. Like Manhattan, London is increasingly become for the very rich.

Most Punk landmarks have long disappeared. The Roxy Club is now the basement of a shoe shop, in the consumerist paradise of Covent Garden. Despite some vestigial grunge, Notting Hill is now associated with young Conservatives rather than the West Indians, bohemians and druggies of yore. The King's Road has become a branded high street, its individuality barely clinging on in the Vivienne Westwood's World's End at number 430. The single best visual record of the London in 1977 can be found in the landscapes of Derek Jarman's film *Jubilee*, with its vistas of corrugated iron and destroyed Victorian housing. Much of it was shot in Rotherhithe, in London's Docklands, which is now one vast new upmarket housing estate. Even Hackney, Throbbing Gristle's nightmarish manor, has become in part a fashionable, art-world district – on the Hoxton/Shoreditch strip. Thirty years on from Punk, London is a city transformed. On the one hand the improvement in housing conditions and facilities can only be applauded, but there is a downside – in that it is increasingly hard for the young, the poor, the bohemian and the artistic to live near the center of town. Which then precludes something like Punk ever happening again. Until the next serious economic downturn.

---

11   See Jean Claude Mension's memoir of the Lettrists, Guy Debord and the Chez Moineau scene, *The Tribe*, San Francisco, City Lights Books 2001.

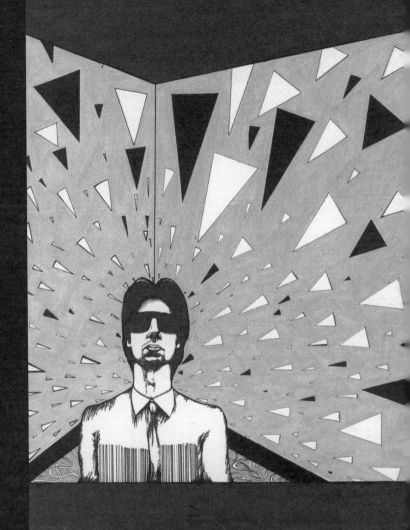

Jon Savage, *Mono*, 1977

Debbie Jubilee at the shop Seditionaries in front of a
blow-up of the bombed city of Dresden, approx. 1976

Jamie Reid, *God Save The Queen*, 1976

Vivienne Westwood, Malcolm McLaren, *Rape*-T-shirt, Seditionaries, 1976

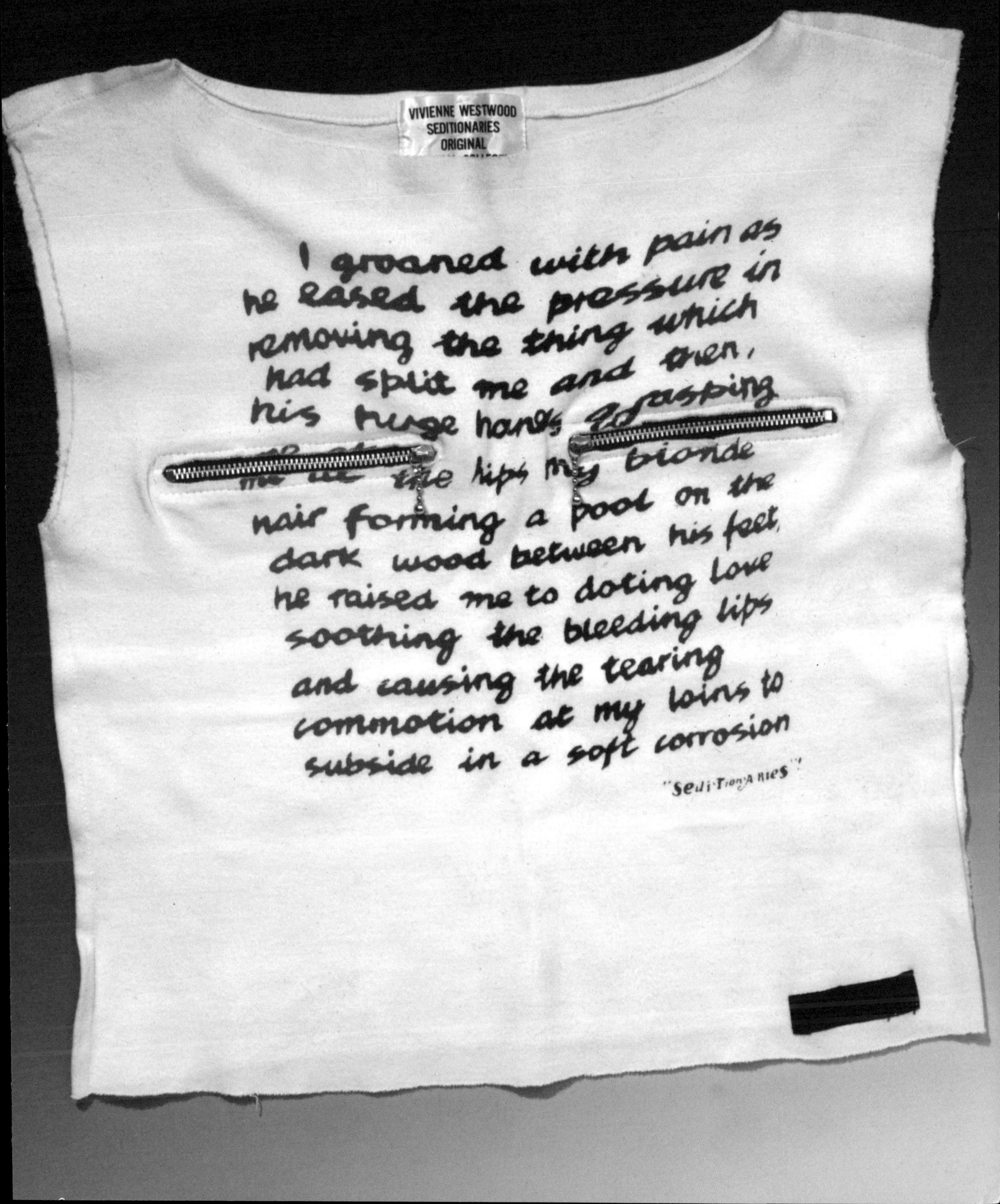

I groaned with pain as he eased the pressure in removing the thing which had split me and then, his huge hands grasping the lips my blonde hair forming a pool on the dark wood between his feet, he raised me to doting love soothing the bleeding lips and causing the tearing commotion at my loins to subside in a soft corrosion

"SediTionARIES"

VIVIENNE WESTWOOD
SEDITIONARIES
ORIGINAL

Jordan with a friend in front of the shop Sex, 430 King's Road, 1974

William English, *Vivienne Westwood,* in the shop Sex with fetish mask, approx. 1975

William English, *Vivienne Westwood*, in the shop Sex wearing the Venus-T-shirt, approx. 1975

William English, *Vivienne Westwood,* in the shop Sex wearing a rubber durex cat suite, approx. 1975

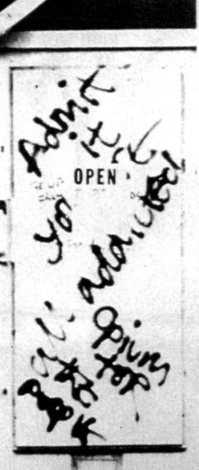

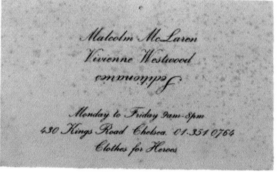

Vivienne Westwood, Malcom McLaren, business cards, Sex, 1974 & Seditionaries, 1975

King's Road shop Seditionaries, 1976

"Hello Joe, been anywhere lately
Nah, its all played aht Bill,
Gettin too straight"

Vivienne Westwood, Malcom McLaren, Two Cowboys, T-shirt-motive, Seditionaries, approx. 1976

Debby Jubilee in the shop Sex in front of blow-up of the Piccadilly Circus, 1976

Genesis P-Orridge, *It's That Time of the Month*, from *TAMPAX ROMANA*, 1976

Genesis P-Orridge, *Venus Mount*, from *TAMPAX ROMANA*, 1976

Genesis P-Orridge, *Pupae*, from *TAMPAX ROMANA*, 1976

Derek Jarman, *Jubilee*, 1977, stills

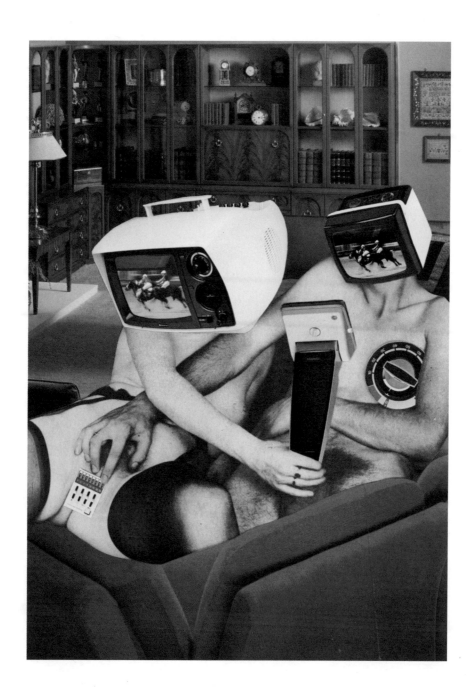

Linder, *Untitled*, 1977

Linder*, The Secret Public/another music in a different kitchen*, 1978

another music in a different kitchen

BUZZCOCKS

Linder, *Untitled*, 1977

Linder, *Untitled*, 1977

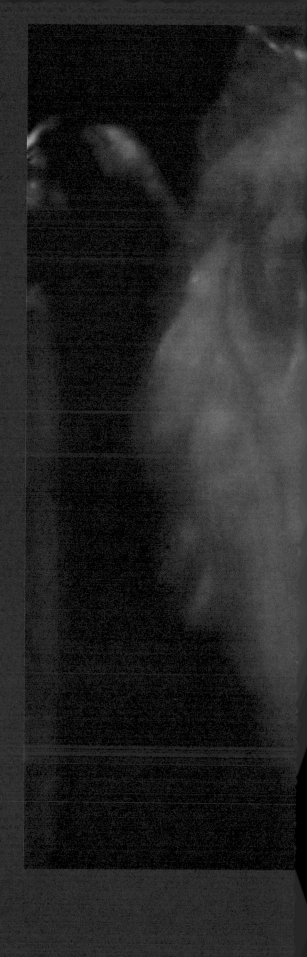

Linder, Ludus concert, La Hacienda club, Manchester, 1982

```
can I see me
I throw up screens
I am messy
```

```
it is not I
who seeks the fool
it is the fool
who seeks I
```

Linder, *SheShe*, 1981

.come find me when I'm hiding
hiding but still not knowing

am I your death
behind my flesh
does my skull smile

life is too short
still we make a show
we are unhealthy and fragile
we are unhealthy and fragile

Bill Woodrow, *Car Door, Armchair and Incident*, 1981

Johnny Rozsa, *Leigh Bowery with Trojan, Pakis from Outer Space*, 1983

Johnny Rozsa, *Leigh Bowery with Trojan, Pakis from Outer Space*, 1983

Johnny Rozsa, *Boy George*, 1978

Johnny Rozsa, *Steve Strange,*

Talking Heads, 77, 1977

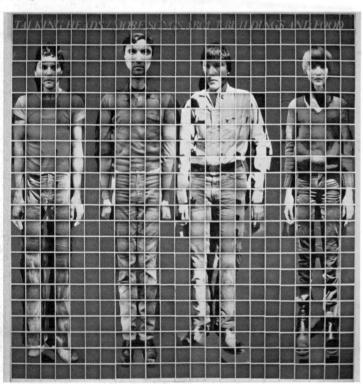

Talking Heads, *More Songs About Buildings and Food*, 1978

i can't seem to face up to the facts
i'm tense and nervous and i can't relax
i can't sleep because my bed's on fire
don't touch me i'm a real live wire

psycho killer
qu'est-ce que c'est?
fa fa fa fa fa fa fa fa fa far better
run run run run run run run away

Psycho Killer, **Talking Heads**

New York Dolls, *Too much too soon*, 1974

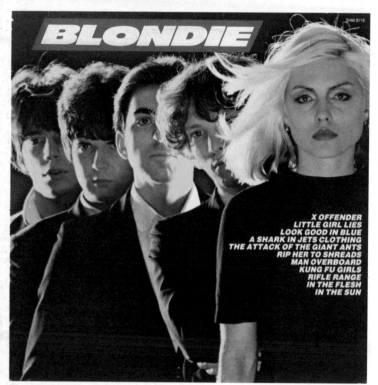

Blondie, *Blondie*, 1976

what i want
i want now
and it's a whole lot more
than 'anyhow'
i want to fly
fly a fountain
i want to jumpjumpjump
jump a mountain

See no Evil, **Television**

*i was sayin let me out of here before i was
even born – it's such a gamble when you get a
face
it's fascination to observe what the mirror does
but when i dine it's for the wall that i set a place*

*i belong to the blank generation and
i can take it or leave it each time
i belong to the _____ generation but
i can take it or leave it each time*

Blank Generation, Richard Hell & The Voidoids

Contortions, *Buy*, 1979

James White and The Blacks, *off white*, 1979

Lydia Lunch, *Queen of Siam*, 1979

jesus died for somebody's sins but not
mine
meltin' in a pot of thieves
wild card up my sleeve
thick heart of stone
my sins my own
they belong to me, me

people say beware!
but i don't care
the words are just
rules and regulations to me, me

Gloria, Patti Smith

Punk is New York, New York is Punk

Glenn O'Brien

What is Punk art? That's about as complicated as what is Punk music, and it's more subtle and elusive. But whatever Punk rock was, at the outset, had a lot to do with art. And if there is such a thing as Punk art it shares certain qualities and values with the rock 'n' roll of a certain time and a certain attitude.

Punk evolved in New York City in the seventies, but nobody called it Punk then. Punk music grew out of the downtown scene, out of bands living in lofts or tenements of New York, which was then the undisputed art capital of the world, not just center of the art market but the center of art production and the crest of the wave of the future. The seventies art world was miniscule compared with today's titanic multi-billion dollar network. The market was small and artists didn't get into the profession to get rich or famous, at least not in the same way we think of those things today. It was an undefined, idealistic and almost naive moment, when pop, abstraction, conceptual art and hard edge lived side by side, sometimes griping and sniping but mostly peacefully co-existing in a non-commercial bohemian bonhomie. If there was an "us-versus-them," it was the artists against bourgeois culture, not the conceptualists against the painters. And at night the artists went out to see their neighbors play some rock 'n' roll at a loft party or a boho bar.

I remember a band called the Artwisers that used to play some nights at an art world hangout, the Lower Manhattan Ocean Club, where Patti Smith and Talking Heads played some of their first gigs. They were called the Artweisers, which I guess was half art and half Budweiser. They weren't very good but maybe they were the first Punk band in a way – existing to entertain artists in an art neighborhood, and not pretending to be more than that. New York in the seventies was nothing like the city of today. I remember running for my life with a poet friend, from guys with knives while walking home from the Ocean Club, maybe after hearing the Artweisers. New York was cheap and filled with people making art and music. The city was a joke on late night TV and the joke was about muggings and a Wild West atmosphere that seemed to America like anarchy on its doorstep. In 1975 the city was facing bankruptcy and then President Gerald Ford declined assistance, leading the *New York Daily News* to headline: Ford to City: Drop Dead. That was the way the U.S.A. looked at its cultural capital. An alien environment. The East Village looked like Berlin after the war. One of the only thriving businesses was heroin. But there was plenty of vitality left in the city. Rents were low and the art world was well entrenched in the abandoned industrial spaces of Soho, Noho and the Bowery. Artists could live and work here with a part time day job.

It seemed to happen that the artists and the musicians rubbed (and bent) elbows quite naturally. The vortex of cutting edge culture was the bar called Max's Kansas City whose regulars included many artists, poets and musicians among other brands of bohemian. A community of artists drank there every night, mostly gathering in the front near the bar, a crowd that might include John Chamberlain, Forrest "Frosty" Myers, Larry Poons, Neil Williams, Larry Zox, Joseph Kosuth, Donald Judd, Carl André, Les Levine, Larry Rivers, Sol LeWitt, Lawrence Weiner, Dennis Oppenheim, Robert Smithson, Keith Sonnier, and many more. Max's owner Mickey Ruskin would trade drinks for art. The back room was dominated by a red neon work traded to Mickey Ruskin by Dan Flavin against his tab, and was thus named "the bucket of blood." It was a freakier scene, dominated by Andy Warhol and his entourage. Perhaps it was the Warhol contingent, including Brigid Berlin and superstars of all sorts that began to attract a rock 'n' roll crowd which more or less took over the back room, though that didn't drive certain artists away. You might see a Rolling Stone or Janis Joplin or cats from the Jefferson Airplane when they hit town. In the early seventies Alice Cooper, Todd Rundgren and the teenaged New York Dolls were early regulars there. If Punk rock was thought up anywhere, it was probably here on Quaaludes and Singapore Slings.

Meanwhile the Warhol Factory's house band, the Velvet Underground, took up a residency upstairs at Max's in the summer of 1970, while downstairs owner Mickey Ruskin was trying to kick the Dolls out. Of course they wound up playing there after the Velvets left. New York was a smaller scene then, and it was certainly big enough that the artists and the musicians could have hung out in different bars, but they didn't. People liked it that way. The artists and musicians liked the mix. The musicians wanted to be taken seriously like the artists. The artists wanted groupies like the musicians. A merger was in the works. During the sixties rock 'n' roll had been transformed by a mass culture of psychedelics into something resembling a religion, acquiring atmospheric trappings from eastern religions, and pretentious ambitions related to classical music and opera. But in New York rock musicians didn't "set the controls for the heart of the sun" or imagine strawberry tinged aquarian utopias the way their peers on the coast or in Britain did. Perhaps it was the grittiness of the city, but the bands here had a nourish realism to them. Punk would appear not as a descendent of hippie but of beat. It wasn't about the cosmic transcendence of acid or the militant naturality of marijuana but about the rush of amphetamine and the anodyne oblivion of junk. The Velvets understood noise, and their early alternative to the bluesy "rave-ups" of British blues were cacophonous explosions of feedback and smashing glass that owed more to the most out free jazz than to country blues. The new New York bands would be like the artists they mixed with: abstract, minimal and pop.

The Velvets and The Stooges made city music for city people – fast, loud and rude. The New York Dolls were something new, a blues based band with New York schtick. At first they seemed almost a deliberate satire on the Stones. Mick Jagger and Brian Jones had taken sexual ambiguity pretty far, but the Dolls went over the top, dressing in semi-drag, mixing ladies high heels and platforms with jeans and Cub Scout uniforms. David Johansen's rubbery rouged lips seemed even bigger than Mick's and Johnny Thunders seemed even more junked out than Keith. The Dolls were the first rock band to totally embrace camp, and their peculiar blend of Bo Diddley, the Shangri Las and over-cranked amps produced a music that was generally perceived as unspeakably bad. It was said that the Dolls couldn't play. In fact they simply put out such a mixed message that what they were doing was hard to hear; except for the kids. The Dolls were ignored in their own country, but a tour of England infected the island nation with their aesthetic and it would bounce back to America as the second British invasion. They were such a

hit with the London cognoscenti that no less than pre-Pistols Malcolm McLaren signed on as their manager, believing that by packaging them as communists in red vinyl he could break them in the States. By then Punk was about to hit and the end, for the Dolls, was near.

I first saw the Dolls at the Mercer Arts Center, an art space that housed The Kitchen and venues like The Oscar Wild Cabaret, where in February 1973 the Dolls staged an evening called *The New York Dolls and All Their Friends*, the latter being Suicide, Jonathan Richman and The Modern Lovers, and Wayne County. These were all bands that played for the art world, as were the others who frequented that venue, like Ruby and the Rednecks, Chelsea Girls' star Eric Emerson and his Magic Tramps, and the Harlots of 42nd Street. We didn't know Punk was being invented. For a minute it was called "glitter rock." Then one night the Mercer Arts Center, the home of the new music as well as much of the city's experimental theater and performance collapsed in a heap of rubble. It seemed like an omen.

But the next generation of performers emerged from that art world vortex. Patti Smith was a beat influenced poet who lived with the young artist Robert Mapplethorpe and sang about Jackson Pollack. Her act evolved out of readings at Max's and other art world venues. She dated Tom Verlaine, whose name was a tribute to the Rimbaudian aesthetic on the rise and his band Television featured a poet named Richard Hell on bass and a jazz-trained drummer. Their music sounded like they never heard blues. I first saw them upstairs at Max's. They were being managed by a guy who had briefly edited Warhol's *Interview* and who may have sold some Warhol's made by someone who took Andy literally when he said "anyone could make my paintings."

The Ramones were the other crucial determinant of the Punk musical aesthetic. Dressed like hustlers out of a Warhol film (and the characters in their song *53rd & 3rd*) they created a new sound—tight, stripped down and above all fast. I once asked Debbie Harry "What is Punk?" and she answered without missing a beat: "Punk is a time signature." The Ramones created that time signature, distilling rock to its quintessence and playing songs in under two minutes. Overnight the guitar solo was out of business.

But these musical mutations didn't occur in an aesthetic vacuum. They happened in a community of art students, sexual minorities, self-exiled Midwesterners, and refugees from the old world. These post-Pop kids didn't know the world before Warhol, before Campbell's soup was art. And while they might have looked poor and tough, they knew what art was all about. They weren't theorists, they were believers and doers. As soon as there was a new venue at clubs like Max's and CBGB's there was an explosion of bands in New York, then everywhere within amplified earshot. And they weren't clones. Dozens upon dozens of bands were created that had something new, a schtick, a gimmick or a dream. New clubs popped up – Mudd, Danceteria, Tier Three, the Pyramid and many more – and those clubs were packed, even if the audiences were mostly other bands, artists and their entourages. Suddenly there was a community with a little music scene and art world of its own. New artists made the record sleeves. The fifth Ramone was their own art director, Arturo Vega.

They had learned about bad from Warhol – how the easy way out could be more interesting than Hollywood technique. Out of focus, out of synch. Even the safety pin, which came to symbolize Punk, can be traced back to Warhol. A 1966 photo shows the artist in a leather jacket and futuristic looking wraparound sunglasses with several safety pins hooked to his jacket. Apparently he wore them as an improvised brooch, based on the practice of fashion window dressers – a job once done by him, Johns and Rauschenberg too. Daring to be bad showed cool; they loved Amos Poe's film *Blank Generation* and its live performances by Blondie, the Ramones and the Talking Heads, so out of sync you weren't even sure it was the right song. John Lurie, attempting to reinvent jazz, essentially a moribund form, created a spectacularly re-imagined variety with his band The Lounge Lizards, but treated it dismissively. He said that when he called it "fake jazz" in an interview, he ruined the next ten years of his career. The Punk moment was not a guarded one. Of course the lumpen punker didn't know about all his of these cultural precedents. Even if he did, he didn't let on he knew much of anything. He

wanted to be sedated. The Punk pose was contrarian and his motivations and influences were for him to know and you to find out. But the Punk intelligentsia was a hard core of artists by any means necessary. An informal council of secret chiefs held the key knowledge and that was casually transmitted to the community on a need to know basis.

The artist who probably had the most direct impact on Punk was Chris Burden whose performances had a profoundly inspiration effect on the Punk generation. To name a few there were *Shoot* (1971), in which he had himself shot in the arm with a 22 rifle, *Deadman* (1972), in which he lay down on La Cienega Boulevard in Los Angeles under a tarpaulin, *Trans-fixed* (1974) in which he was nailed to a Volkswagen, *Doorway to Heaven* (1973) in which he risked death placing live wires to his chest, and *747, January 5, 1973* in which he fired several shots with a pistol at a Boeing 747 approaching Los Angeles International Airport. Burden was willing to risk his life for art. And everything about him, from his radically clean cut look, with close cropped hair, Ralph Nader suit and tie, and innocent face, prefigured the styles and attitude of punks to come. One of his performances was actually titled after a particularly radical Velvet Underground song *White Light/White Heat*. Modernism had a long tradition of provoking outrage and outrage must constantly renew itself. The public was outraged by Pollock presenting what everyone's child could supposedly do as advanced art, by Warhol and Lichtenstein presenting the commonplace as the same. More desperate times called for more desperate measures and the Punk spirit inspired new tactics, like blatant imitation. Fuck originality! Mike Bidlo not only repainted Jackson Pollock's oeuvre but he staged a performance of himself as Pollock pissing in a Peggy Guggenheim's fireplace, before moving on to a remake of the Warhol Factory.

Many of the key figures of the period were musicians and visual artists simultaneously. Painter and filmmaker James Nares was a member of painter and filmmaker John Lurie's band that became the Lounge Lizards, as well as a member of the original Contortions, which at one time or another included new cinema actors Bradley Field and Christian Hoffman, and later Pat Place, also a visual artist. David Wojnarowicz played in the band 3 Teens Kill 4 and made confrontational paintings and collages, many dealing with the systematic oppression of gays. Filmmaker Jim Jarmusch played in the Del Byzanteens. Jean-Michel Basquiat formed the band Gray and for a while Vincent Gallo, then a painter, played in that band which, though essentially unschooled, created a sophisticated, compelling sound through techniques borrowed from minimalism and Miles Davis, and instinctive use of electronic instruments. Perhaps today Basquiat is too pricey to be connected with "Punk art," but his practice was as wild and impudent, as any artist's. He attracted attention through his SAMO© graffiti, but Basquiat was never a graffiti artist in the conventional sense. He didn't work the trains, but mostly Soho, the gallerists' neighborhood, and the East Village, home of his peers. SAMO© works were not just "tags" or decorated signatures – they were statements or slogans designed to intrigue. When he actually began to paint, using impoverished materials and found objects, he displayed phenomenal vision. His paintings had a Punk attitude and with their revisionary history, absurdist humor and outsider beauty, they captured the elusive spirit of the moment. Basquiat's favorite peer, Keith Haring, was also a strategic practitioner, using graffiti's techniques to present a new style work.

Colab (aka Collaborative Projects) was a loosely artists collective (that included filmmakers and writers) organized to promote collaborative work. Among its accomplishments were the creation of the New Cinema theater, and the influential 1980 *Times Square Show*, a large group art exhibition staged in an abandoned porn site. That show included painting, graffiti, performance, film and video. The setting was perfect because the participants were truly a band of marginalized outsiders. Many of the same artists formed the core of the *New York New Wave* show organized by Diego Cortez in 1981.

The New Cinema (a tiny venue at 12 St. Marks Place in the East Village) was short lived but it was as close to a real, coherent movement as anything in the Punk era. It didn't codify a canon, as Dogma would, but it had a strong, specific aesthetic that came out of the French New Wave and its influences. Like the music scene, where the bands' audiences were mostly other musicians, these filmmakers tended for their films to one another, and the community of musicians and artists provided actors for one anothers films. The big stars of the Punk cinema were Eric Mitchell, John Lurie, gallerist Patti Astor (the Fun Gallery,) Lydia Lunch, David McDermott, and René Ricard who began as a Warhol superstar, appearing in four films from 1965 to 1967, and he returned to stardom in Eric Mitchell's *Underground U.S.A.* Outside of that group a whole scene popped up, with such filmmakers as Beth and Scott B., Anders Grafstrom, Amos Poe, Betsy Sussler, and Liza Bear.

As a critic René Ricard was crucial to the early success of Julian Schnabel and Jean-Michel Basquiat, but his greatest contribution was when he began to paint his poems he created a form of his own, which he continues to practice. Alan Vega, the singer half of the crucially important group Suicide, has been making sculptures as long as he has been making music. Suicide was the first of the New York electronic bands and they created a compelling, pulsing, super loud music that was danceable but as hard in its own way as more traditional lineups like the Ramones or Blondie. No band was louder or more electrifying. I remember standing just inside the door at CBGB's to protect my ears, yet they are still performing and Vega is still exhibiting his cool, funky sculptures.

Punk art, if there was such a thing, was antimovement. It wasn't made by joiners but quitters. It was more important to be different than to share a style. Energy and independence were more important than an identifiable direction, which is the challenge that any art you might call Punk still poses to traditional ideas of modernism. At the time that Punk happened – or new wave or no wave – names invented to mitigate the unfortunate connotations of Punk – musicians and visual artists faced similar obstacles in showing and selling their work. Both record companies and art galleries preferred one big artist to ten smaller artists who might sell the same volume. In such a situation formula trumps creativity and even novelty. And so in the late seventies and early eighties artists and musicians found few channels open to their work, so they made their own outlets, their own small record labels and galleries.

A wave of home made music labels appeared, demonstrating that they could find artists and develop and sell them. And with the Soho scene unreceptive to what younger artists were doing, new galleries popped up like mushrooms all over the East Village. The work showed by these galleries was often exciting and innovative and tended to be at odds with mainstream critics and academics and even the secondary market. Young people, it seemed, were not excited by work steeped in theory. If you had to read the essay to appreciate it, maybe there was something lacking in the stack of lumber on the gallery floor. Painting, which had been declared dead, was suddenly in the forefront. The new art world wanted art that was more artistic. It wanted easels, berets and absinthe, muses, jazz and drug addiction.

What is Punk? In its time Punk was not so much an ideology as a resistance to ideology. It wasn't an aesthetic but an independence of fixed aesthetic. In its earliest use (16th century?) a punk was a prostitute. More recently a punk was a jailhouse catamite. But by the time that music given that label, Punk derived from Hollywood usage, meaning a wise guy, an upstart, a nobody pretending to be somebody.

The term Punk was not often heard during the period now known by that name. It probably got attached to the music through *Punk Magazine*, the small but brilliant periodical put out by cartoonist John Holmstrom, writer Legs McNeill, and photographer Roberta Bayley, who worked the door at CBGB's. That magazine was based on a small community and its tastes were insular. It was mostly about the CBGB's world and the Ramones, Blondie, the Dictators and a handful of other groups. Lou Reed was looked up to and the Sex Pistols were regarded with enthusiastic curiosity. To the British Punk was a movement. It had very specific aesthetic parameters, musically and visually, probably because the Brits do so love to class people. The music was clearly inspired by the styles of the New York Dolls and the Ramones, but the fashion was utterly original to London. New York, of course, loved the Sex Pistols, as it loves anything wild, and it even loved The Clash who sang about being bored with the U.S.A., but

the internationalization of the musical style, and the definition of the visual style, turned Punk into something very specific. As soon as someone could say something wasn't Punk, it was over. It was probably an advertising copywriter at Sire Records, which has home to both the Ramones and the Talking Heads, who came up with the term New Wave, to explain the obvious difference between the art school trained Talking Heads and the loud and fast boys from Queens. It echoed the French nouvelle vague, which worked pretty well, but it didn't mean much, at least in New York. But people start believing what they read and so there was New Wave. And then there was the No Wave, an insiders' joke on new wave, but which effectively described the bands, filmmakers and personalities who were both intellectual and nihilistic, revolutionary but elitist. The No Wave seemed to sense early on that in the future what was known as Punk would be loud and fast and dumb, defined by the rules that came over with the British Punk bands and the aesthetics of the Ramones – cartoony and semi-ironically dopey. But the loud and fast and negative style was henceforth what Punk would be seen as, so it was time to make a distinction. The No bands were something else. They weren't the musical hall; they were art. Or a hybrid thereof. James Chance was the Mick Jagger, James Brown, Iggy Pop and Ornette Coleman of the No Wave. His bands, the Contortions, then James White and the Blacks and the Flaming Demonics, mixed funk, rock, jazz and attitude to create a new kind of fusion – you could dance to it or have a nervous breakdown to it. James was sometimes cool, blowing his sax with articulate abandon, and sometimes hot, taking Iggy's audience interaction into attack mode. If he didn't like the looks of someone in the audience he might go after them.

Many characters contributed to a time, a spirit, an attitude, an evironment to which you could apply that still amusing, slightly worn yet undefinable four letter word. A combination of funk and puke. But as crucial as it was, one of those turning points in culture, it is still misunderstood, even by those who should know better.

Spike Lee's 1999 film *Summer of Sam*, which is about New York in 1977 (the summer of Son of Sam), depicts CBGB's in the year the Ramones,

Blondie and Talking Heads had hits. What's strikingly wrong is that the club patrons are all dressed in leather and safety pins and have dayglo fanned Mohawks. It wasn't until Wendy O. Williams and the Plasmatics hit the airwaves in 1981 that this self-caricature would be become popular. By 1999 Punk, the original self-caricaturing scene had become so confused with its caricature that it was no longer anything resembling the complex, multivalent matrix that originally earned the appellation. No Wave was a perfect kiss off to the whole flawed idea of Punk, and in retrospect it's the real Punk.

When I think about Punk I think about Iggy Pop ending a song and yelling "Did you like that?" and the audience cheering and Iggy shouting "Let's do it again!" and repeating the same song. I think of when the USDA took Romilar CF cough formula off the market Steve Mass, the owner of the Mudd Club went to the drug store and bought all they had left and served it that night at the second floor bar. And, also at the Mudd club, I remember early on James Chance's brilliant and beautiful girlfriend and manager Anya Phillips, wearing a slashed-up evening gown, leapt from the bar, attacked a girl on the dance floor and slapped her silly. When I asked her what happened she said, "I didn't like the way that bitch was dancing." That, to me, was art.

Robert Mapplethorpe, *Patti Smith*, 1976

Robert Mapplethorpe, *Patti Smith*, 1978

Robert Mapplethorpe, *Patti Smith*, 1978

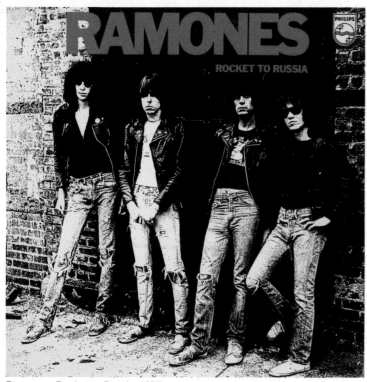

Ramones, *Rocket to Russia*, 1977

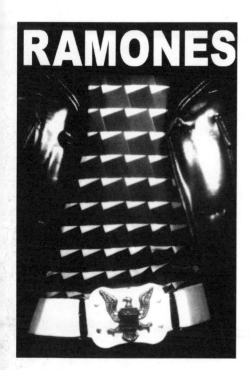

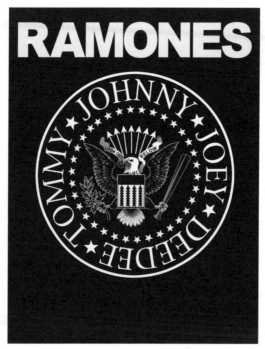

Arturo Vega, Ramones Poster, 1975

Arturo Vega, Ramones Logo, 1976

Arturo Vega, Silver Dollar

Arturo Vega, Ramones Eagle, 1977-89

Robert Longo, *Joanna*, 1983

Robert Longo, *and Larry*, 1983

Robert Longo, *Jonathan*, 1988

Lynda Benglis, *Artforum Advertisement*, 1974

Vito Acconci, *Under History Lessons*, P.S.1, Long Island City, New York, 1976

Christy Rupp, *The Rat Patrol*, 1979

112

Richard Hambleton, *Shadow Man*, New York City, East Village, 1982

David Wojnarowicz, from *Arthur Rimbaud in New York*, 1978–79/2004

Richard Kern, *Fingered*, 1986

Mark Morrisroe, *Untitled (Hello from Bertha)*, approx. 1983

Mark Morrisroe, *Untitled (Jason Skiper on the morning of his father's wedding)*, 1985

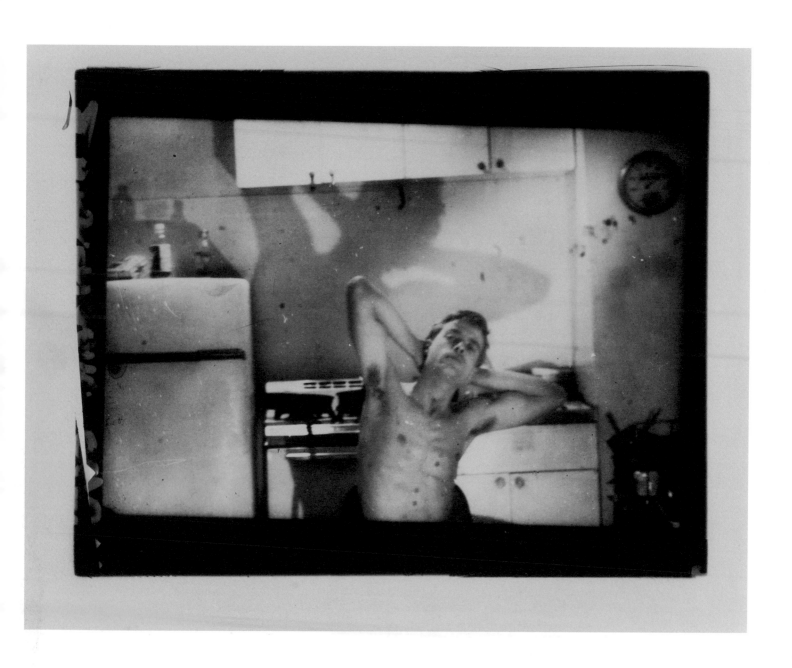

Mark Morrisroe, *Untitled (Michael Walsh at home in the kitchen),* 1987

Mark Morrisroe, *Untitled (self portrait with blue and white wig)*, approx. 1984

Mark Morrisroe, *Untitled*

Mark Morrisroe, *Untitled*

> Mark Morrisroe, *Untitled (La Môme Piaf)*, 1982

>> Mark Morrisroe, *Untitled*, 1982

Tony Oursler, *The Loner*, 1980

Tony Oursler, *The Loner*, 1980, stills

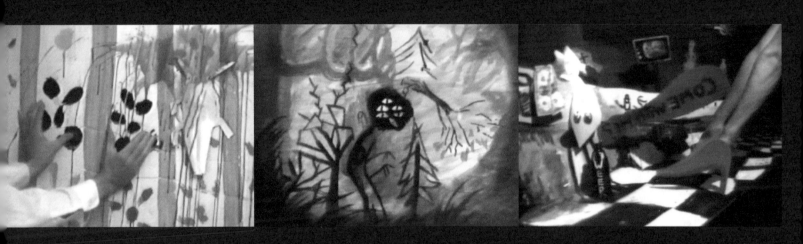

Ann Magnuson, *Made for TV*, 1984, still

Ann Magnuson and Tom Rubnitz, 1984

Alan Vega, *Alan Suicide, American Supreme 2*, 1976/2001

ghostrider motorcycle hero
bebebebebebebe he's a-screamin' the
truth
america america is killin' its youth
bebebebebebebe he's a-screamin' away
america america is killin' its youth
america america is killin' its youth
ghostrider
ghostrider

Ghostrider, Suicide

Mania D, *HERZschlag*,1980

dicht unter der haut
du brauchst dick're nadeln als ich
gier! / gier! / gier!
tausend tote tiere
mitten im kopf
gier! / gier! / gier!
ich gier nach dir
gier nach dir
gier nach drogen
gier nach fleisch
gier nach dir
tanz debil / tanz debil / ganz debil

Tanz Debil, Einstürzende Neubauten

MALARIA!

Malaria!, *New York Passage*, 1982

ich seh' deine braunen augen
dein braunes haar
wie lang und schön
oohhhh
nur noch eine stunde
an deinem munde
und dann mußt du gehn

geh duschen geh duschen
ab in die fabrik
geh duschen geh duschen
wart ich komm mit

Geh Duschen, Malaria!

aufstehn/hinlegen
verbrannte erde
ich steh auf viren
ich steh auf chemie
aufstehn
abstürzen
einstürzen
in die luft sprengen
krieg unter autos
ich steh auf feuer
ich steh auf rauch
ich steh auf krach

Steh Auf Berlin, Einstürzende Neubauten

Einstürzende Neubauten, *1/2 Mensch*, 1985

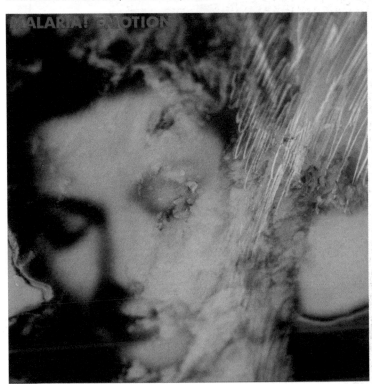

Malaria!, *Emotion*, 1982

DIN A TESTBILD
Programm 1

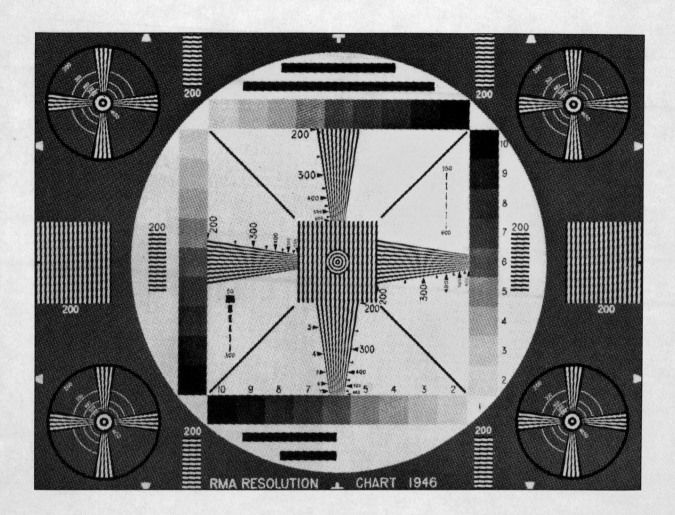

DIN A Testbild, *Programm 1*, 1980

der rhythmus
des herzmuskels
lässt das blut
stoßweise
aus der offenen
wunde
schießen
nylonstrümpfe
werden steif
durch getrocknetes blut
das taktgefühl
geht im krieg
verloren
lieber gar kein herz
als ein herz
aus paprika

Rhythmus im Blut, Die Tödliche Doris

Chaotic Holidays

Wolfgang Müller

Punk In General

Order and disorder

In the early 1980s, a Punk band with the peculiar name KUKL descended on West Berlin. They played at Kuckuck (cuckoo), a cultural centre near the bombed out ruin of Anhalter Bahnhof railway terminus. Kuckuck was a squat, one of a total of 170 that eventually existed in the western part of the city. Directly opposite lay a fenced-off plot strewn with rubble that had been reclaimed by nature since 1945: creepers, acacias, birch trees, undergrowth and tall grass. From early spring each year, a nightingale would sing here at deafening volumes. It sang to mark its territory, and it sang to drown out the noise from the street beyond the fence. The wasteland itself was crisscrossed by amateurishly levelled "streets" where drivers without a license could practise. The proprietor of the Autodrom, as it was called, was Harry Toste, also known as "Straps-Harry" (Harry suspenders), a transvestite with long, dyed-yellow hair and bright green knee-length stockings held up by a red suspender belt. Later, he was sometimes to be seen at Café Anal, a gay and lesbian Punk bar in Kreuzberg. In 2004, Harry died aged 97.

In 1987, more widespread attention was focussed on this overgrown plot of land by an exhibition called *Topography of Terror* and, after several failed attempts, building work on a museum of the same name finally began there in the autumn of 2007. Here, on Prinz-Albrecht-Straße, was where Himmler, Heydrich and Kaltenbrunner sat at their desks, at the nerve centre of the Nazi regime of political crimes and repression: the headquarters of the Gestapo, the SS and the Reich Security Main Office.

Places in transition

This, then, was the setting in which the Punk band KUKL played their concert. They didn't draw much of a crowd, in spite of being from Iceland – or precisely because of this fact.[1] The band's singer was called Björk and the audience of no more than twenty people included the writer Max Goldt, who recalls a woman coming back from the toilet just before the gig started: "This place is disgusting!," she said, "There's a pregnant twelve-year old in there, and she's pissing standing up!"[2]

Björk had already caused a stir in Iceland by appearing on stage in an advanced state of pregnancy. An eye-witness from Reykjavik, the then 14-year-old Mohican-sporting punk Jón Atlason, later described this event in an article for the *tageszeitung*.[3] Today, Jón lives in Vienna and works as a lector for Icelandic at the university. And Björk is a global megastar who opened the 2004 Olympic Games in Athens. Without Icelandic Punk, no one would refer to the Danish-Icelandic artist Olafur Eliasson as an Icelander. Since Punk, Icelanders are also allowed to be musicians and artists, not just writers like before.

Occupied spaces, material and immaterial

But what spaces did Punk open up on the frontline in Berlin? The heavily subsidized western half of the city was governed by a conservative political caste who were not only fighting the Cold War against the East, but who also faced a hostile young population of its own consisting of drop-outs, freaks, anarchists and conscientious objectors. While rents ran at near unaffordable levels, property speculators allowed many houses to fall into disrepair. In spite of this, Berlin's media showed little understanding for the resulting wave of squatting, focusing instead on "protection of property." Finally, Berlin's mayor Eberhard Diepgen coined the term "anti-Berliners" for all those he considered part of the alternative milieu. This was a rich breeding ground, then, for all manner of "parallel cultures".

In many cases, the people squatting the vacant properties were poor students and the proactive unemployed. When art students occupied and renovated a house belonging to art collector Erich Marx, Joseph Beuys, whose work Marx collected, came out in their support and donated drawings for a "solidarity" exhibition. This atmosphere saw

---

1   Long into modern times, Icelanders were considered extremely unmusical: "for the Icelanders sing very badly, with neither tact nor merit." Quoted from *Letters from Dr. Uno of Troil Concerning A Journey To Iceland Undertaken In The Year Of 1772*, Uppsala and Leipzig 1779.

2   Max Goldt, *Wenn man einen weißen Anzug anhat*, Berlin 2002, p. 86.

3   Jón Atlason, "Frech wie Freydís," in *taz Magazin Dossier*, 20 April 2002, Berlin.

the emergence of the alternative daily newspaper *tageszeitung*, many fanzines,[4] underground galleries, cinemas, clubs and small independent record labels.[5] The scene drew on a wide range of groups: post-hippy alternatives, sneeringly referred to by the punks as "Mueslis;" young men who refused any form of military service and who came to Berlin because the city's inhabitants were exempt; and activists from the women's, lesbian and gay movements.

Back then, the singer of Berlin band Didaktische Einheit (didactic unit) would perform wearing nothing but a golden jockstrap.[6] Today, Hans-Werner Marquardt is senior arts editor at *BZ,* a Berlin subsidiary of Germany's biggest selling tabloid, the *BILD-Zeitung*. Today, the pet punks of Germany's yellow press are Campino and Ben Becker, following in the footsteps of the late lamented entertainer Harald Juhnke. Most of the squats have been legalized, often purchased by the squatters themselves.[7]

The real and/or fake Heino

But were Campino and his band "Die Toten Hosen" (the dead trousers) ever really Punk? Or was it more a question of hairstyles? In any case, just how decisive a hairstyle can be is illustrated by the story of their regular support band, the "real Heino". For many years, Norbert Hähnel, owner of the "Scheissladen" (shit shop) record store in Kreuzberg, took to the stage as a clone of the German popular singer Heino,[8] sporting his trademark dyed blond hair and big sunglasses. In 1982, filmmaker Rainer Werner Fassbinder bought LPs and homemade tapes from the Scheissladen for a film project.[9]

The biography of the "real Heino" sounded plausible enough: he, Norbert Hähnel, was in fact the

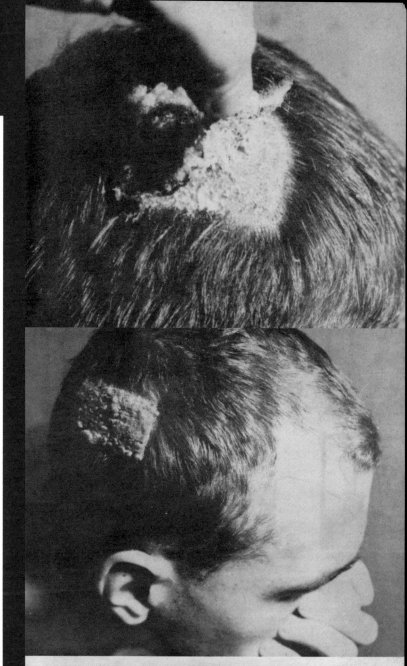

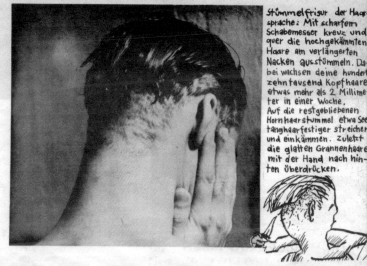

Stümmelfrisur der Haarsprache: Mit scharfem Schabemesser kreuz und quer die hochgekämmten Haare am verlängerten Nacken ausstümmeln. Dabei wachsen deine hunderttausend Kopfhaare etwas mehr als 2 Millimeter in einer Woche. Auf die restgebliebenen Hornhaarstummel etwa See tanghaarfestiger streicher und einkämmen. Zuletzt die glatten Grannenhaare mit der Hand nach hinten überdrücken.

Die Tödliche Doris, *Die Meta-Punk-Frisur: eingelegtes Teppichstück im ausrasierten Haar*, from the album booklet *Boingo Osmopol*, 2, 1981

4   See: www.punkfanzines.de

5   Germany's first independent label, David Volksmund Produktion, was founded in 1971 by Berlin band Ton Steine Scherben.

6   Wolfgang Müller, *Geniale Dilletanten*, Berlin 1982, p. 91.

7   Martin Büsser, "Über die Verwurzelung 'extremer' Musik in der bürgerlichen Kultur und den 'Extremismus' des Mainstream", in *testcard 16, Extremismus*, Mainz 2007, pp. 20f.

8   Jello Biafra of punk band the Dead Kennedys collects Heino records as a document of just how low music can go.

9   After Pittigrillis Novel *Kokain*, Fassbinder planned to make a film about the newly emerging scene with music by Étant Donné and Die Tödliche Doris. He died just a few weeks later.

genuine Heino, while the man who performed everywhere as "Heino" was a copy, a fake created by the record company. As Hähnel explained, he, the "real Heino," had refused to play in South Africa as long as the apartheid system continued to exist, so the record company had immediately replaced him by a double who was now performing in South Africa under his name. The Real Heino continued with this play on identities until Heino, alias Heinz Georg Kramm, took his unwanted doppelganger to court in 1985. The loser refused to pay the fine and went to prison for several weeks instead. As this example shows, a true punk is dangerous and amusing at the same time. And because s/he wants to experience the here and now not just mentally but also physically, s/he seeks friction, constantly grating against the limits of a freedom that is supposedly boundless.

Speichel and Margot

In East Berlin, too, there were many examples of subversive and affirmative playing with reality. In the scene centred on the poet Bert Papenfuß, for example, there was a punk by the name of Speichel (saliva/spittle). Speichel called his little dog Margot, the first name of East Germany's Minister of Education, Margot Honecker. "Come on, Margot, sit! Good dog, give me a paw!" What grounds were there for any GDR police officer to arrest Speichel? In a documentary film, East German punks tell how they hired a Russian luxury car, a Volga, and drove in full get-up, with dyed hair and dog collars, onto the marketplace of a small town where a May Day parade was taking place. They wound down their windows and waved red flags at the baffled speakers on the platform. The speakers, rendered speechless by such behaviour, waved back.[10]

In its 1987 edition, the East German dictionary of popular music finally included an entry on Punk. The phenomenon was portrayed as a consequence of the capitalist system: unemployment and a lack of prospects = Punk. Logically enough, the entry failed to mention a single East German Punk band. It also included a typo that turned the "anti-capitalist West Berlin Punk band" Die Tödli-

The youngest punk in town: Oskar Dimitroff (2), in: *Das Leben des Sid Vicious*, Super-8-film, Die Tödliche Doris, West Berlin 1981, based on an idea by Max Müller.

che Doris (deadly Doris) into "Die Tödliche Dosis" (a lethal dose) – a stroke of genius![11]

Aesthetics and resistance

In the East, as in the West, the officially recognized protest movement was represented by bearded guitar-playing bards. But East Germany's best-known exemplar of this type, Wolf Biermann, whose personal contacts to Margot Honecker can only be described as an open secret,[12] hardly matched the aesthetic of the Punk rebellion. In 1976 he was invited to give a concert in Cologne by Jakob Moneta, after which he was expelled from the GDR. Had he referred in his music to his former relations with East Germany's Minister of Education, by forming a band named Love & Loathing In The Nomenclature for example, Biermann might even have become part of the then emerging Punk movement.[13] Visceral loathing was a big theme in Punk, as reflected in band names like Rotzkotz (snot puke), Kotzübel (gonna vomit) or Brechreiz (nausea). But the loathing of Punk

10 Ólafur Sveinsson, *Schräge Zeit*, documentary film, D-IS 2004; in 1987, a punk called Jan from the band "Demokratischer Konsum" (democratic consumption) married an Icelander to escape East Germany.

11 Peter Wicke, Wieland Ziegenrücker, *Rock-Pop-Jazz-Folk – Handbuch der populären Musik,* Leipzig, DDR 1987, p. 374ff.

12 In 1953, aged 17, Biermann moved from Hamburg to the East Germany on the initiative of Margot Honecker.

13 "When, one evening, Biermann said how revolted he was by the folds in the skin on Margot's neck – she was by now married to the chairman of the East German State Council, Erich Honecker – Sigi (Moneta's partner) was disgusted by this machismo and wanted to throw him out." in: *Schröder erzählt*, part 3, Berlin, April 2002, p. 27f.

focussed more on the slippery-smooth body of the bourgeoisie and its loathsome character traits: opportunism, hypocrisy, self-righteousness. With Biermann now acting as a committed advocate of George W. Bush's Iraq War and receiving an honorary citizenship from the City of Berlin for his courage and spirit of resistance, it's high time a monument was erected to the unknown East German Punk.[14] In the GDR, s/he was excluded from any kind of career and quite likely to be arrested at will and imprisoned for months. But as a consequence of this subversive and affirmative play with reality, the political impact and aesthetic influence exerted by Punk in the GDR are not only underestimated and denied, but all-too-often quite simply overlooked.[15]

Swastikas: taboo and provocation

Besides Betoncombo (concrete combo),[16] Die Ärzte (the doctors) from West Berlin[17] are still considered *the* authentic German Punk band. In the early 1980s, they featured in Jörg Buttgereit's splatter films. Amateur Super-8 films enjoyed cult status in the Punk scene and were screened in makeshift cinemas like Frontkino, Risiko, KZ36 and KOB. Here, first steps were ventured into zones of radically subversive form that had been considered taboo in Germany up to that point. In the Punk scene, Germany's past resurfaced in entirely new form. Nazi symbols were appropriated and given new meanings. Sex Pistols bassist Sid Vicious pointed the way, marching down Parisian boulevards in a swastika T-shirt in Julian Temple's *The Great Rock 'n' Roll Swindle* (1979). In West Berlin in 1982, Jörg Buttgereit made Germany's first Hitler movie, *Blutige Exzesse im Führerbunker* (Bloody Excesses in Hitler's Bunker) that aimed to be neither a documentary, nor an educational feature film, nor a mystic artwork. Buttgereit's film is totally disrespectful, pure trash.

"The younger ones among you might not recog-

Scandalous: The crocheted doll and post-punk Wollita (18), made by Françoise Cactus.

nize me...," says Adolf Hitler, played by the "real Heino," as he launches into a monolog. A reanimated Eva Hitler, née Braun, then castrates and chops up her lover, helped by a "Germanic breeding bull" cobbled together out of severed body parts, played by Buttgereit.[18]

In another cult film of the period, Sid Vicious was seen walking the streets again in a swastika T-shirt – in West Berlin, played by Oskar Dimitroff, aged two.[19] In 1982, film critic Dietrich Kuhlbrodt, who at the time also worked as a lawyer at Hamburg's regional court responsible for prosecuting crimes dating from the Nazi period, presented Buttgereit's Super-8 film to readers of the *Frankfurter Rundschau* newspaper, and later discussed it as an alternative to the epic *Der Untergang* (The Downfall: Hitler and the End of the Third Reich, 2004).[20]

Breaches of taboo: from subversion to affirmation

Neo-Nazis and "Mueslis" alike found it hard to deal with this radically subversive mode of appropriating Nazi symbols. While Jörg Buttgereit acquired a deeper knowledge of the field, becom-

14 Or to Speichel and Margot.

15 Roland Galenza, Heinz Havemeister (eds.), *Wir wollen immer artig sein, Punk, New Wave, Hiphop und Independent-Szene in der DDR 1980-1990*, Berlin 2005. Boehlke, Michael, Henryk Gericke, Too much future, OST-PUNK, Berlin 2005. Alexander Pehlemann, Ronald Galenza, Spannung, Leistung,Widerstand – Magnetbanduntergrund DDR 1979 – 1990, Berlin 2006.

16 See also Frieder Butzmann, *Die Musik in Geschichte & Gegenwart*, first supplementary volume, Berlin 2008.

17 Former members of Soilent Grün.

18 The title of "Germany's first Hitler comedy" was later falsely claimed by the marketing campaign for Dany Levy's *Mein Führer: The Truly Truest Truth About Adolf Hitler* (2007).

19 *Das Leben des Sid Vicious*, Super-8-film, Die Tödliche Doris, 1980. Lead role played by Oskar Dimitroff, son of Tödliche Doris drummer Dagmar Dimitroff (1960–1990). "17.9.1977. Stasi arrests 17-year-old Dagmar Dimitroff for showing her own paintings at a Pankow fleamarket without permission. She also campaigned on behalf of Wolf Biermann. After ten months in prison, she was released and sent to West Berlin." Stiftung zur Aufarbeitung der SED-Diktatur, Berlin 2002.

20 Dietrich Kuhlbrodt, *Deutsches Filmwunder:* Nazis immer besser, Hamburg 2006, pp. 60ff.

ing an expert on horror and monster films, action artists like Christoph Schlingensief and the painter Jonathan Meese were later to draw on Punk's legacy of taboo-breaking and genre games. As "neo-punks" or "art rebels," they now affirmatively fill the void in postmodernity which the West covers up with its claim to absolute superiority: It's all just a game of signs and symbols – nothing is forbidden! But Punk's impact on society is deeper than such an outcome would suggest. Thanks to their fast, friendly assimilation into the mainstream, the neo-punks were left with little time to use the experience of the past as a basis for an updated subversive aesthetic pointing beyond the endless round of forced scandals. The fact that Schlingensief now paints a bit like Meese and Meese produces plays at the Volksbühne theatre in Berlin reflects a superficial arbitrariness and interchangeability. The outer forms of subversion and affirmation are subject to constant change: Today, with the prevalent gesture of refusing all limits to personal self-realization, the "Punk" label somehow seems to fit everyone.

There's Punk, and then there's Punk: Wollita, the (post-)punk

In 2004, Berlin's tabloid newspapers BILD and BZ aimed their biggest guns at an alleged "exhibition of child pornography"[21] at Kunstraum Kreuzberg. Their main target was a life-size crocheted doll by the name of Wollita made by Françoise Cactus[22] who based the figure on an advertisement for commercial sex taken from the BZ: "Horny woolly mouse (18), will do anything!"[23] An absurd hate campaign began that was to last weeks. With worrying success: for the first time since 1945, a group of organized young Nazis demonstrated in the Kreuzberg district. Their banners and flyers reproduced the tabloid media's headlines and calls for the exhibition to be closed immediately: "If 'art' is suited to awakening the perverse fantasy of child molesters, then this 'art' should be banned!"

Two years later, a production of Ideomeno at the Deutsche Oper opera house in Berlin was taken off the bill due to fears of an Islamist threat. Worried about the state of our freedom, BILD, BZ and Tagesspiegel newspapers asked prominent public figures to comment. Christoph Schlingensief's response: "We can't approach a culture that's 500 years younger than Christianity and demand: off with the burqa, on with a miniskirt, on the double."[24] Instead of analyzing "our" paranoia and talking about its consequences, then, Schlingensief inscribed himself into a mainstream that likes to demonstrate the boundless freedom of the "civilized West" by displays of naked female flesh. In 2007, the BZ awarded its culture prize to the "art rebel" Jonathan Meese.

For years, the post-punk BZ media victim Wollita has been fighting to receive this same award – as modest compensation.[25] In the meantime, she's even had an elegant evening burqa crocheted specially as a way of giving the culture vultures at BILD and BZ access to entirely new intellectual and aesthetic insights and horizons.

"Punk's not dead!" shouted Berlin's punks defiantly. But its survival depended on post-punks finding new modes of body awareness and constantly rethinking what could be done with hairstyles. In some cases, "Punk" even became invisible, manifesting itself as a naked, crocheted doll, or as a gentle, revelatory elf.

Punk In Detail

The most creative period for Punk in West Berlin was between 1979 and 1984. On the one hand, there were the "hardcore punks" and their bands like Betoncombo and Ätztussis (corrosive chicks). And on the other a sprawling, more experimental music scene made up of young artists and intellectuals. In Berlin, these scenes overlapped, mixed and cross-fertilized to a far greater degree than they did elsewhere, and the romanticizing accounts contained in certain books of hard-fought street battles between different groups

---

21   The exhibition When Love Turns To Poison focused on the dark sides of love and sexuality.

22   Françoise Cactus formed the band The Lolitas in Kreuzberg in 1985, and later Stereo Total.

23   Stéphane Bauer (ed.), Bild – Macht – Rezeption. Kunst im Regelwerk der Medien, ID Verlag, Berlin 2005.
Stéphane Bauer (ed.), Wollita – Vom Wollknäuel zum Superstar, die Biografie, Berlin 2005. http://fm4.orf.at/zita/208579

24   And he went on: "As a Christian, I no longer have to go to confession. A few drops of holy water are enough, I can relativize as much as I like, it's second nature to us." Tagesspiegel, Berlin, 27.9.2006.

25   "Wollita muss den BZ-Kulturpreis bekommen!" http://www.martin-schmitz-verlag.de/Wollita/Buch.html

are perhaps a little exaggerated.[26] There was a wild mixing of scenes that met in bars and clubs, occupying new spaces with names like Chaos, Risiko, Shizzo, Exzess, Dschungel, Frontkino, KOB, Penny Lane, SO 36, and in the late 1980s Kumpelnest 3000 and Ex 'n' Pop.

Red roses – with thorns

In the stuffy, decrepit West Berlin of the 1980s, the party never stopped. It was the only city in Europe without a curfew. At four one morning, I sat with the East Berlin writer Heiner Müller in Kreuzberg's proletarian late-night bar Rote Rosen,[27] where "East Müller" and "West Müller" chatted about the festival of "Geniale Dilletanten" (brilliant dilettantes). This event, held on 4 September 1981 at the Tempodrom, a large circus tent next to the Berlin Wall, drew a crowd of over 1,200. This success came as a surprise, as the scene which assembled on stage for the first time that evening was disapproved of and rejected by professional rock musicians: all the dilettantish noise bands that developed out of West Berlin Punk. The bill included Gudrun Gut from the band Malaria!, Frieder Butzmann, DIN A Testbild, Einstürzende Neubauten, Christiane F., Die Tödliche Doris, Frank Xerox (now known as DJ WestBam). Filmmaker Wieland Speck, now director of the Panorama section at the Berlin Film Festival, emceed *Die große Untergangsshow* (The great Destruction Show). Three years previously, he had appeared as a hustler in the last film with Marlene Dietrich, *Just a Gigolo*. From the front row, Dr. Motte[28] threw full beer cans at the emcee. One can even say, then, that the roots of techno and the Love Parade were present here, even physically present. Much of the music produced on stage sounded terrible, shabby, amateurish and unprofessional; homemade instruments or therapeutic screaming to point of hoarseness, punctuated by sea shanties sung off-key by Zwei Mädels und das Meer (two lasses and the sea). In spite of this, the musical soup that was served up proved to

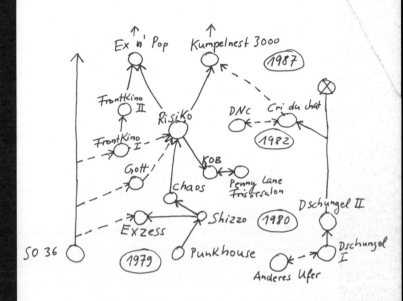

Bars, pubs, discotheques: fluctuation within West Berlin's punk scene, sketched by Wolfgang Müller, 1990.

be substantial and not without consequences.[29] In his diplomatic bag, Heiner Müller smuggled back twenty copies of the *Geniale Dilletanten* manifesto (published by Merve) and handed them out in Prenzlauer Berg. They fell on fertile soil, as improvisation was in vogue in East Berlin at the time, with experimental bands often making their own instruments out of leftovers and playing with junk and scrap metal.

Glam and glitter

Glam rock and the opening up of gender boundaries and sexuality are further elements that flowed into Punk. As the first gay bar in Europe to show itself without bricked up windows and without bouncers, the café Anderes Ufer (the other bank) opened in 1977 on Hauptstrasse in the Berlin district of Schöneberg. David Bowie and Iggy Pop lived right next-door, at number 155.[30] Like Heidi Paris and Peter Gente from the Merve publishing house, they often visited the café, sometimes bringing French philosopher Michel Foucault with

---

26   Jürgen Teipel, *Verschwende deine Jugend*, Frankfurt: Suhrkamp, 2001.

27   Red Roses on Adalbertstraße in Kreuzberg.

28   Co-founder (in 1989) of the Love Parade, then using his real name, Matthias Roingh, and playing in the band DPA (Deutsch-Polnische Aggression).

29   *Die große Untergangsshow, Festival der Genialen Dilletanten*, Friedrichshafen 2005.

30   The Berlin years, 1976 – 1978.

Thirty years on, Berlin 2008: Klaus Theuerkauf (endart) and "Ratten-Jenny," the woman who beat up Martin Kippenberger in 1978

them. The painter Salomé reflected the erotic atmosphere when he performed half naked with his band Geile Tiere (horny beasts) at the Dschungel club. With hindsight, his performance, in which he played a "bitch" taking Luciano Castelli for a walk on a leash,[31] appears as a queer version of Valie Export's famous walk with Peter Weibel on a dog lead.[32] Though revolutionary in the act of running a gay bar in full view of the public, the organizers were less adventurous in their aesthetic tastes. The old, sperm-crusted sheets hung on the walls as relics by Blixa Bargeld were removed immediately, as were the unwearable designs from his boutique Eisengrau – ultra-loose-knit pullovers, or were they just full of holes? Salomé's water-lily paintings were better received. Not far from the Selbsthilfegalerie (self-help gallery) on Moritzplatz, the centre of the Neue Wilde group of neo-expressionist painters including Rainer Fetting, Elvira Bach, Bernd Zimmer and Helmut Middendorf,[33] Klaus Theuerkauf opened his endart gallery on Oranienstrasse, Kreuzberg's main drag, celebrating something that was perceived by the scene as "Punk art": not certainty and the propagation of truth, but the creative shaping of destruction. Paint, trash, obscenity and transgressions of the limits of political decorum were used to create

something that set West Berlin (then "the heroin capital of Europe," as Bowie later stated) quite clearly apart from other cities.

Punk meets art
Oranienstrasse was also the address of the Punk club SO 36. In 1978, the leaseholder Martin Kippenberger entered into a fateful but now legendary "dialog with the youth" of the day. When he raised the price of tickets and drinks, he had to face "Jenny The Rat," an encounter during which she demolished his face. He photographed his bandaged head and titled the work: *Dialog mit der Jugend* (Dialog With The Youth of Today). He then moved to Paris, where art didn't collide so heavily with punk.[34] In fact, Kippenberger conducted the first direct dialog between art and Punk, as Jenny The Rat was actually just three years his junior.

Berlin realism
The glowing reputation of Berlin's diverse independent music scene soon spread beyond the city limits. Even the fusty Berlin senate eventually realized this and appointed a "commissioner for rock" with a budget for funding bands. In most cases, the lucky newcomers vanished as quickly as they had appeared. As in East Berlin, the art institutions in West Berlin followed the official line. In both halves of the city, this almost always meant realism: socialist realism in the East, critical or neo-expressionist realism in the West. The few exceptions included Galerie René Block, founded in 1964, showing work by artists like Joseph Beuys, Gerhard Richter, Sigmar Polke and Nam June Paik. There was also Galerie Gianozzo, Galerie Jes Petersen, Galerie Eisenbahnstraße[35] and Künstlerhaus Bethanien, where "non-realist" artists were offered a platform. From 1981, Ursula Block's gallery GELBE Musik (yellow music) brought together fine art, Punk, New Music and avant-garde. It is regrettable that the Berlinische Galerie, a museum specialized in art made in Berlin, purchased hardly any key documents, no performance or concert videos, no Super-8-films or artworks from the Punk or "Geniale Dilletanten"

31 Salomé, *Japanese bitch on a walk with her dog*, 1981.

32 Valie Export, *Aus der Mappe der Hundigkeit*, Vienna 1969.

33 Frank Apunkt Schneider, *Als die Welt noch unterging*, Mainz 2007, pp. 65f.

34 Jenny The Rat moved to London.

35 Hans-Christian Dany, Bettina Sefkow, Ulli Dörrie, *Dagegen – Dabei, Strategien der Selbstorganisation seit 1969. Teufelsaustreibung im Kohlenkeller*, Hamburg 1998, pp. 149ff.

scenes. The East Berlin scene was luckier in this respect, as the Leipzig gallerist Judy Lybke carefully put together an archive of all her underground Super-8-material after the demise of the GDR in 1989.[36]

Nina Hagen, Punk icon

The expulsion of Wolf Biermann generated a mood of resignation in East Germany. His stepdaughter Nina Hagen also left the GDR, moving to London. Her achievements include reconciling the "alternative" and Punk scenes in the West. In her music, she mixed the demands of the women's movement for increased self-determination with insolent "Fuck Off!" gestures à la Punk. Although her music overall was conventional and eclecticist, she became the face of Berlin Punk in the arts and society pages of the broadsheets. In an interview, she revealed that her role models included Valeska Gert, who played Mrs. Peachum in the 1931 film of *The Threepenny Opera*. And Hagen's hairstyle, black lipstick, make-up, gestures and use of grimaces really are very reminiscent of this impressive dancer, writer and artist.

Punk Past and Present

Valeska Gert: ur-punk

Valeska Gert was Berlin's first punk, a proto-punk. In the 1920s, she danced procurers, prostitutes, traffic – a cinematic choreography. While Hitler published *Mein Kampf* (my struggle), the title of her first autobiography was simply *Mein Weg* (my path).[37] Valeska Gert worked with G.W. Papst and experimental filmmaker Walter Ruttmann. She called for music consisting of nothing but noises.[38] In its time, with its proto-fascist fetishization of the harmony of physical forms à la Leni Riefenstahl, her grotesque dancing must have been perceived as alien or incomprehensibly subversive. For the Dadaists, Valeska Gert was far too prosaic, too direct; for the Surrealists, she was too

Nina Hagen's role model: ur-punk Valeska Gert dancing *Berlin Underworld* in 1934 in London

conscious, too concrete. For both, she was probably too emotionally physical and obscene – at least for a *white* woman. In a diatribe from Goebbels' propaganda ministry about "degeneration" in modern art,[39] she is the only German Jewish woman artist cited, and her "grotesque dance"

36 A long text about the West Berlin punk and dilettante scene appeared in *monopol*, 5/2005, Berlin: Die Frontstadt by Cord Riechelmann, p. 18–31; at the same time, the first documentation of West Berlin's underground Super-8-film and music scene appeared with the DVD/CD/book *Berlin Super 80*.

37 Valeska Gert, *Mein Weg*, Leipzig 1931.

38 Ibid. "I want to have a new music that consists of sounds from reality. This music can only come to us via movies or radio, the noises should not be imitated but taken from real life, merely assembled by the artist." pp. 44f.

39 Frank-Manuel Peter, *Valeska Gert, Tänzerin, Schausielerin, Kabarettistin*, Berlin 1985, Abb. S. 74–75.

gets two mentions. She was late in emigrating to the USA, where she immediately clashed with the organization of exiles that called on her in a letter not to make hateful remarks about her country of asylum. Her reply: I didn't hold my tongue in Germany under the Nazis, so why should I keep quiet in a democracy? In New York she ran The Beggar Bar.[40]

From Beggar Bar to Goat Stall

After the war she returned to the destroyed Berlin and opened Die Hexenküche (witch's kitchen) in the west of the city.[41] In *KZ-Aufseherin Ilse Koch*, she danced and sang a female concentration camp guard, a number that was thirty years ahead of its time. The West Berlin audience, she complained, only wanted to see Social Democrat, anti-Communist cabaret. The authorities, too, harassed her wherever they could. Frustrated, she moved to the North Sea island of Sylt and opened Der Ziegenstall (the goat stall), a bar whose interior would not have looked out of place in a 1980s Punk club: straw in cribs, old furniture, graffiti. At the Ziegenstall, as the landlady approvingly noted, the guests bleated and were milked. She was offered cameos by Federico Fellini[42] and Rainer Werner Fassbinder.[43] In 1975, Ulrike Ottinger made the experimental film *Die Betörung der blauen Matrosen* (bewitching the blue sailors) with her and Tabea Blumenschein, and in 1977, Volker Schlöndorff made a documentary about her life.[44] Immediately after Valeska Gert's death in 1978, her heir, the journalist Werner Höfer, had the Ziegenstall demolished. Her papers, already thrown out as trash, were rescued at the last minute.[45]

Pogo dancing, Berlin style

The pogo is a Punk dance where the dancers leap up and down and collide with each other in mid air, and one might say that Valeska Gert invented a Berlin version of it. With her reflection of the present, which she expressed directly in and with her body, and with her irreverent approach both to the canons of art and to the predominant ideals of physical beauty of her time, Valeska Gert is usually referred to today as a dancer. This is a simplification, as she could equally be seen as a precursor of performance art, as a living sculpture, or as a unique total art work. In November 2006, a small street in Berlin's Friedrichshain district was named after her. On Sylt itself, there is no memorial to this outstanding artist.

Chaotic Holidays on Sylt

Walter Benjamin describes the specific changes in body awareness in big cities, where sensory perceptions must be instrumentalized and organized to a huge degree to guarantee survival in an accelerated everyday environment.[46] Punk is an attempt to feel and become aware of the body and its interactions with its surroundings in a different, direct way. Including the insight that permanent disorder is necessary. Without awareness, no friction.

Today, the island of Sylt with its masses of tasteless, postmodern holiday homes and pressure to conform is quite barren in aesthetic and material terms. When German Railways launched its promotion campaign for a cheap "Weekend Break" ticket, the authorities on Sylt fought hard against it – for fear of an invasion of less well-off tourists. They demanded that the special offer should exclude the island, linked to the mainland by the Hindenburgdamm. This had consequences: on 27 March 1995, hordes of punks stormed Sylt to hold their "Chaos Days." "Punk's not dead!" they chanted. The island's mayor, shopkeepers, and cultural officials were appalled by the invasion. Not only does friction facilitate direct physical experience – sometimes art is created in the process.

---

40 Valeska Gert, *Die Bettlerbar von New York*, self-published, Berlin, 1950.

41 It was here that Klaus Kinski gave his first Villon readings.

42 As a factotum in Federico Fellini's film *Julia Of The Spirits*, IT 1965.

43 Rainer Werner Fassbinder, *Acht Stunden sind kein Tag*, 5-teilige Familienserie, TV Produktion 1972.

44 Volker Schlöndorff, *Nur zum Spaß, nur zum Spiel*, D 1977.

45 Valeska Gert's estate is now kept at the Akademie der Künste in Berlin.

46 Walter Benjamin, *The Work of Art in the Age of Mechanical Reproduction* (1936).

Martin Kippenberger, *1/4 Jhdt. Kippenberger als einer von Euch, unter Euch, mit Euch*, 1978

THIS MAN IS PLAYING ON LUXUS

KIPPENBERGER

S.O.36 RECORDS

Martin Kippenberger, *This Man is playing on Luxus*, 1979

Martin Kippenberger, *This Band is playing on Luxus*, 1979

THIS BAND IS PLAYING ON LUXUS

PHOTO: ARMSTRONG

S.O.36 RECORDS

Autogrammkarte '87: Käthe Kruse, Die Schule der Tödlichen Doris, 1987

Autogrammkarte '87: Wolfgang Müller, Die Schule der Tödlichen Doris, 1987

Autogrammkarte '87: Nikolaus Utermöhlen, Die Schule der Tödlichen Doris, 1987

Die Tödliche Doris, *Chöre & Soli*, 1983

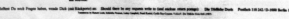

Die Tödliche Doris, *Schmeißt die Krücken weg*, 1987

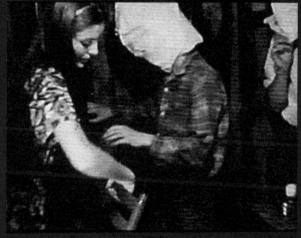

Die Tödliche Doris, *Berliner Küchenmusik*, 1982, stills

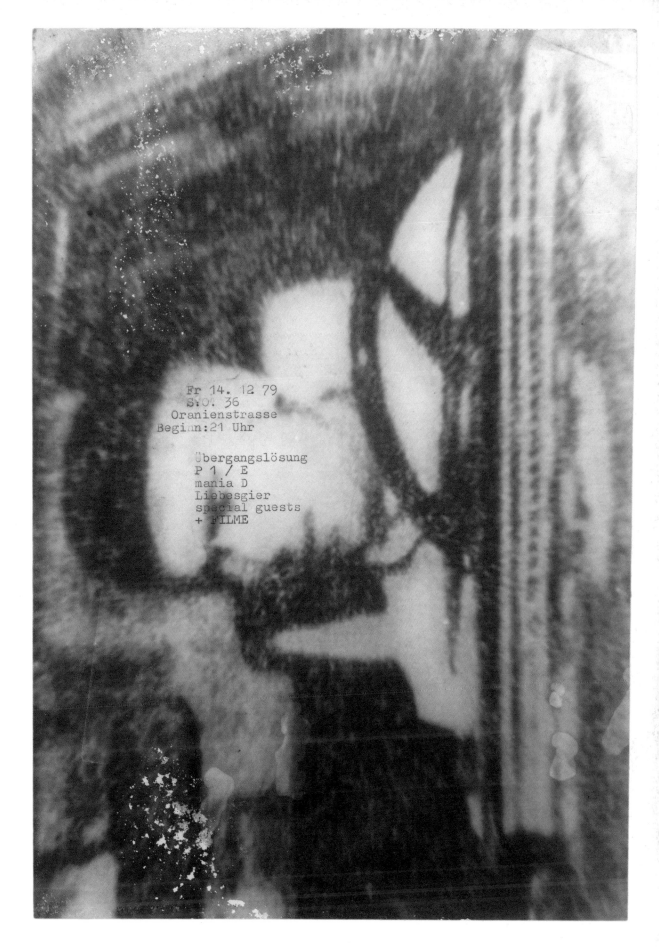

Fr 14. 12 79
S'O. 36
Oranienstrasse
Beginn:21 Uhr

Übergangslösung
P 1 / E
mania D
Liebesgier
special guests
+ FILME

Flyer SO 36, 1979

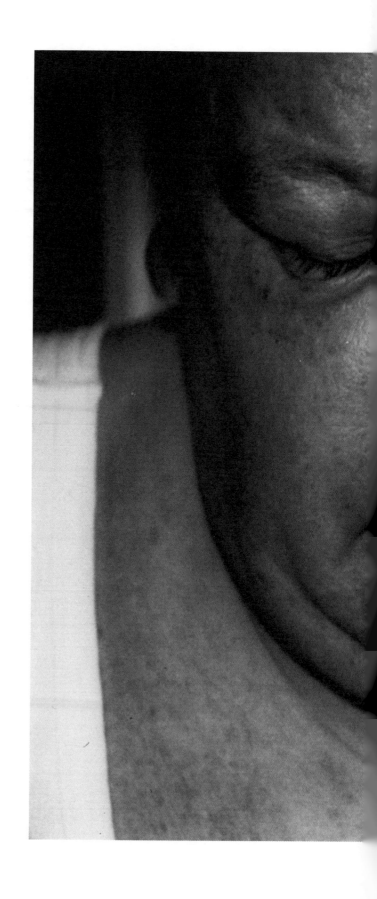

Jörg Buttgereit, *Mein Papi*, 1981

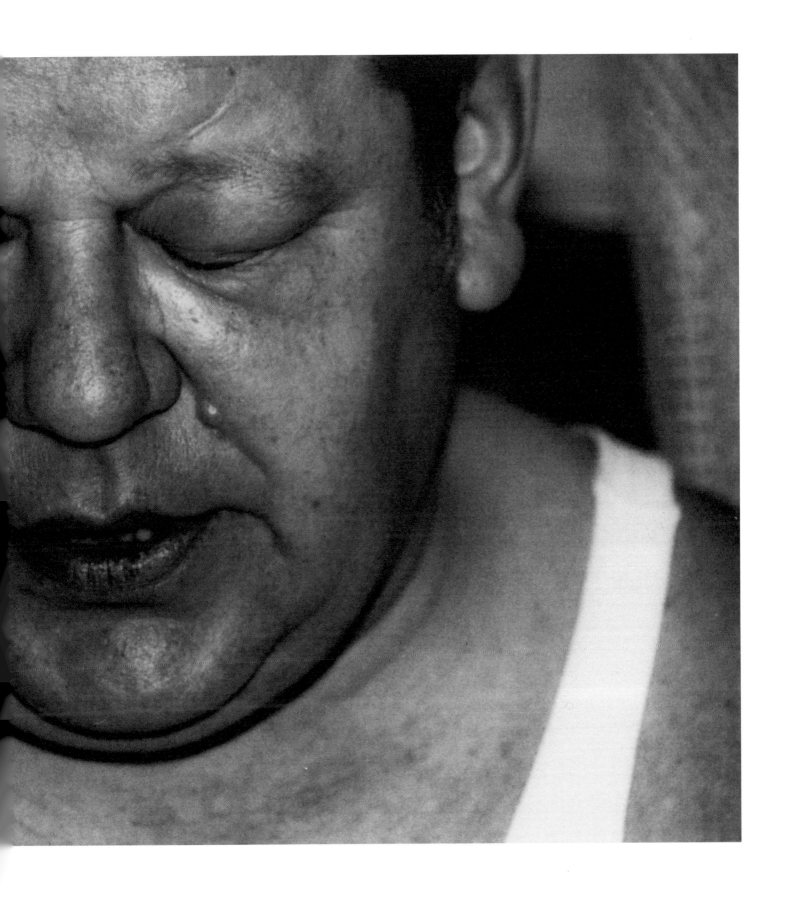

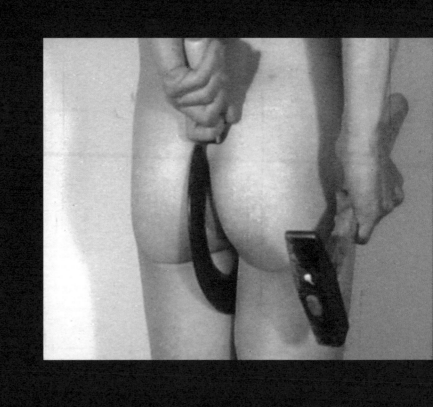

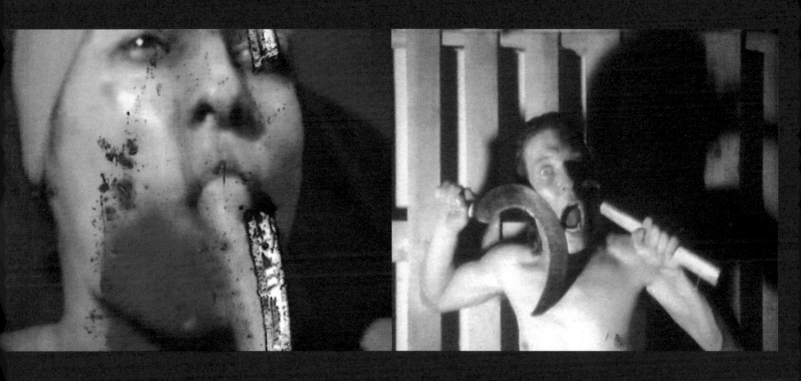

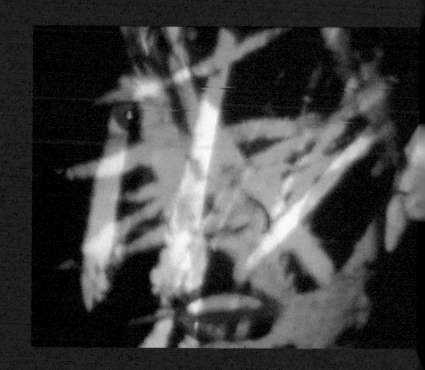

Hormel & Bühler, *Geld*, 1982, stills

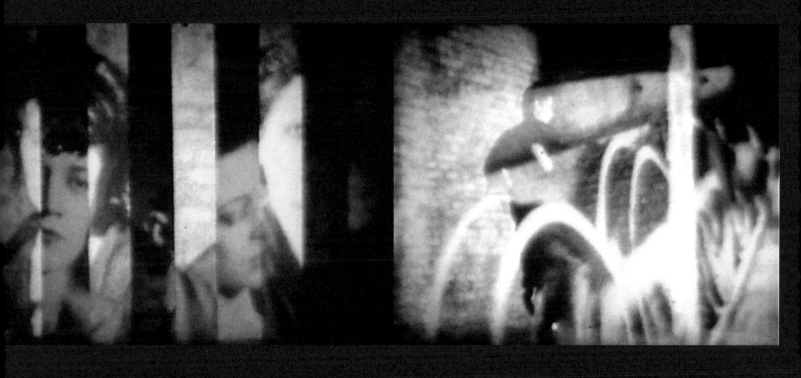

Maye & Rendschmidt, *Ohne Liebe gibt es keinen Tod*, 1980, stills

Notorische Reflexe, *Fragment Video*, 1983, stills

Wolkenstein & Markgraf, *Hüpfen 82*, 1982, still

Sax, 1983, stills

endart, *Die Geburt eines Igels*, 1982

endart, *Tiergarten*, 1985

endart, *Vagina pectoris*, 1984

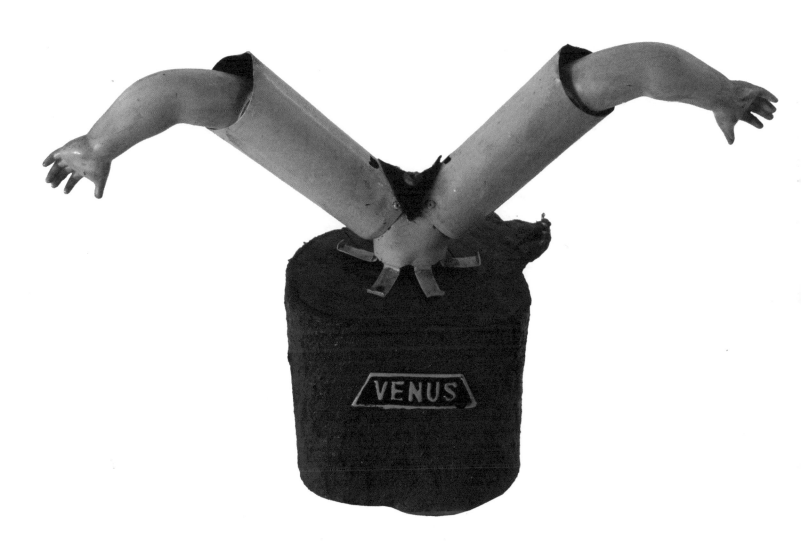

endart, *Venus*, 1984

endart, *god 'n' dog*, 1984

endart, *locus solus*, 1984

Salomé, *Fuck 1*, 1977

Salomé & Luciano Castelli, *Rote Liebe*, 1979

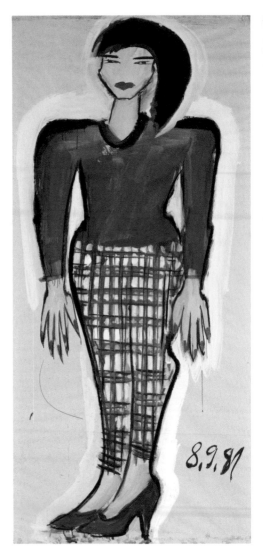

Elvira Bach, *Sechs Tage Budapest,* 1981

11.9.81

12.9.81

13.9.81
Bach

Malcolm McLaren in Conversation with Gerald Matt

The inventor of Sex Pistols and Punk can point to one of the most varied careers – you are an artist, designer, musician and manager. What does Punk mean for you personally?

A way of getting along with myself, a way to express my sexuality, a way to change the culture and in doing so, life. I don't know how else to begin as an artist.

After your studies at several London academies of art you did everything imaginable: there was Let it Rock, Too Fast To Live Too Young To Die, Sex, Seditionaries, World's End, the New York Dolls, Teddy Boys Mode, S/M-articles, and finally the Sex Pistols and Punk fashion. You said once: "The Sex-Pistols were a work of art. My material is neither colour nor sound, but people. I use them, misuse them, manipulate them, because I believe in my idea. The Sex Pistols were an idea, not a band. And they were the most brilliant, most spectacular failure that I ever experienced, simply wonderful." Were all these projects designed to be art?

They could only have been made by an artist. They were ugliness made beautiful. They were intellectually curious, emotionally connected, sexy, subversive and stylish. It was a way of turning art into action.

Back then, in 1974, you went to New York and carried the "Sex Pistols" idea back in your luggage. Why did "cash from chaos" work in London, rather than in New York, the centre of the artistic avant-garde?

I was only meant to stay for a while. It was a break from both Vivienne Westwood and London. I wanted to explore a bigger canvas. But, soon it was time for me to return to the old country. I had venereal disease, powerful ideas and had gained a devastating sense of humor to crush the English with.

What inspired you particularly in New York that you thought would be suitable as an import?

The ability to do anything, whatever it takes. Extremes of behavior. The undying desire to be exploited no matter what. Rock 'n' roll's message was liberating but I never thought the English truthfully believed it. So I was returning to hammer it home.

You have yourself always referred to the strategies of Situationism, Lettrism and Dadaism as well as they were also described by Greil Marcus in *Lipstick Traces*. Did the members of the Sex Pistols band, for example, also use those strategies consciously?

No, these ideas were simply the domain of a few disenfranchised art student friends. The Sex Pistols picked up on the vibe and attitude: the look of it all. And a little of it went a long way. They were simply angry young men in search of an identity and found it in our store, Sex. They wanted to be recognized as legitimate rock stars and all that goes with that. But I, with my art student co-conspirators purposely prevented that from ever happening. This was pure manipulation.

Were Punks paying attention to what was going on in elitist art circles in London, New York or elsewhere?

No. They were too busy dealing with their own vanity – their bodies, dirt. Extreme behavior was all they cared about. They simply didn't want to know about anything other than leaving the 20th century and never return to normal life again. That was their mission. They were elitists and inadvertently, I was responsible for that.

Your creativity in matters of fashion for the boutiques on the King's Road had practically no limits: written on, printed on, torn materials, safety pins, zips, bones, paint and leather, cross and swastika, locks and dog collars … King's Road was in the remotest part of London, a vintage and flea-market paradise. What did the street fashions of McLaren/ Westwood owe to a second-hand culture?

Vivienne was a schoolteacher for little children but loved fashion and shopping for clothes. She was in awe of what she didn't know about: culture – and what that culture could bring to her. I lost my virginity to her at eighteen. Apparently got her pregnant and was finally made responsible and obligated. I was willing prey for her needs. She just wanted to be close to someone who could show her a different way of life – a different way at looking at things. She was too shy and intimidated by culture to understand fully what was going on in the Zeitgeist. She placed culture on a pedestal and I simply wanted to knock it off. I became her rebel art student boyfriend who opened doors that she never knew existed before and dragged her through them. It was a form of education that she had never had. I showed her a way of creating an environment that she could truthfully run wild in. This was what Punk did for her. I fell in love with her for that reason. What she did for Punk was apply her particular skill with my help and vision to making clothes that gave Punk a visual identity before the media even labeled it and the music "Punk." What we in effect did was making clothes that looked wrong. I came from a fashion background. My parents and grandparents were all involved in fashion and naturally, as a teenager, I began to hate fashion for those reasons and was only interested in wearing and ultimately making anti-fashion. We began by digging up the ruins of a pop culture: the authentic remains its outlaw spirit. I had always been obsessed with the look of music and the sound of fashion. This is what I taught Vivienne. I went to art school to be an artist. Not a commercial artist and certainly not a designer. But I had an epiphany when I was very young, when I first set eyes on a Teddy Boy. The air of menace, the brooding figure, his blue suede shoes, showed to me clearly that fashion had power. He was dressed up to mess up. This was something I later came to use when forming the concept behind the store at 430 King's Road Chelsea in 1971.

When I left art school and headed down the King's Road at that time, I simply wanted to be exploited. For this purpose I had carefully made a blue lamé suit copying that very suit that Elvis wore on a cover of an album that I had at home. It was this suit that Vivienne thankfully helped make and I wore it with pride for the occasion. It was a dark, dreary, typical November day in London and I recall walking the whole length of the King's Road hoping someone would notice me, pick me up, take me on an adventure – do something with me! But nobody even paid the slightest bit of attention. However, by the time I got to the end of the King's Road and the clouds above me were about to burst, something happened that changed my life. A man stood in front of me, stopped me in my tracks and after a simple discussion, gave me an opportunity pointing across the road to a tiny hole in the wall of a store. It was here that I began life after art school, at 430 King's Road. It was here that I would find a bridge to cross form art school to the real world and the street. It was here I as an artist would discover how to turn a shop into a painting, an installation, a sculpture … art. Let It Rock was my first incarnation. And then the canvas changed to Too Fast To Live Too Young To Die, and then to Sex and even later, to Seditionaries – all on the same premises. Simply different incarnations. This space was never to be permanent, just a constant changing canvas of ideas. Here on the King's Road where the last dandy of the 60s fell in the gutter, I began my life as an artist in 1971.

I first started working in collaboration with Patrick Casey – someone I admired for his sartorial splendor, an ex-artschool student friend from Chelsea. Not long after, I soon forced Vivienne to give up teaching and work with us. But her relationship with Patrick was not good and so he left. Patrick and I had already begun finding in flea markets the old looks of music. And in my wildest imagination, I then began to tear these clothes apart with Vivienne and re-construct them in a way that I thought was a much better look. Instead of imitating second hand culture, I began improvising around it – turning them inside out and in doing so, presenting them to a more contemporary scene on the King's Road at that time. I simply hated nostalgia and felt it to be just dead tissue. Finally, with a certain confidence, I boiled my ideas down to one word: Sex. Using a phrase from Rousseau, "Craft must have clothes but the truth loves to go naked," I completely repainted and clad the store to look like a sex gymnasium: padded walls, graffitied with salacious writings by Alexander Trocchi and others. I created soft, huge, fat letters in pink vinyl and screwed them to the graffitied Rousseau slogan that covered the façade of the store. It was now called "Sex." I realized that the English are both terrified of and secretly fascinated by sex. I travelled across England to find fetish clothing manufacturers. The Sex store soon became the most extraordinary phenomenon on the King's Road watched by the police, constantly raided. I was often arrested and accused of selling clothes that were liable to cause a breach of the peace. Certain young clients walked out of the store wearing pornographic T-shirts and were immediately arrested. Punk as this look became labeled by the media, was clearly synonymous with free and unbridled sex. It was a liberation. England still kept pop culture at arm's length. I took it as an artistic act of defiance against normal life in the UK and began to destroy all that pretense and culture of deception. The English, I would claim, were a nation of liars whose utter survival depended on how well they practiced this culture of deception. I wanted to make it impossible to return to this way of life again – this "normalness" of England.

In the Traveller Club, a Jazz pub, one could also find artists like Francis Bacon. How did the older generation of artists react to Punk?

Andy Warhol visited my store several times. He fell in love with names like Sid Vicious, Johnny Rotten … and couldn't stop himself from announcing their names. He loved our T-shirts but couldn't understand why I didn't have the name "Sid Vicious" scrawled all over them. That is what he wanted to buy. Francis Bacon on the other hand adored all these young boys in bands. He said Punk was pornography at its best. It was the "laughter of genius, the bathroom of my mind." He only wished, he said, he could have been on the *Top of the Pops*. This was the TV chart show every week on the BBC. David Hockney was later intrigued by it all and when I arrived in Los Angeles. He invited me over to discuss his art, Punk Rock, Vivienne, and his dog, Laurel – named after Stan Laurel of *Laurel & Hardy* fame. Malcolm Morley got me to collaborate with him on a series of lithographs.

At that time the Sex Pistols went to London clubs like Sombrero, Masquerade, Rob's or Louise's. Subcultures of Punk, gay and transvestite groups, unlike anything seen before, came together under the label "Outcast." How did you take to associations of Punk rock and New Romanticism? Was Dandyism an aspect of Punk that is forgotten now?

Punk's dress code was extremely fashion and anti-fashion at the same time. It confused the hell out of the fashion world but they soon were seduced. Deconstruction, Punk's method of design, meant destroying the way clothes were originally made to look. This soon became years later, everyone's fashion directive – a method that was new. From Comme des Garçons back then to Lanvin today, from Jean Paul Gaultier to John Galliano to Vivienne Westwood to Alexander McQueen. The inside-out, upside down, three arms instead of two, slashed, burnt and torn, sleeveless raincoats, bondage trousers, skulls, fetish, the color black, and on and on. It all made up a subversive, sexy and stylish fashion. A fashion that denied itself the right to move. Dandyism as such was always at the top of my list. A priority that forced you to fall in love with yourself. Punk dandies were the rage at Louise's – the lesbian club turned Punk club, where nobody knew exactly what sex anyone was, or cared. Everyone did it all to everyone. Which way, what way. Innocent, or provocative. The look stopped people in their tracks. Virgins looked like sluts. It was a revolution and it appeared unstoppable.

When I met you in New York, you told me how you discovered *Madame Butterfly*. Does opera still have anything to do with Punk, or the way in which it can be used? Was it the theatricality, the pathos or a certain artificiality that attracted you?

Melodrama, simple tragedy, love and death in 90 minutes were all appealing aspects of opera. The pose was everything. The extremes of life were to die for. Punk was always extreme in its youth. It had almost a pre-pubescent tone to it. I do recall twelve year olds being some of the best customers in my shop, Sex, at that time. It was so much a part of one's imagination and it did create a real generation gap that was nothing less than operatic in its extremity.

Why did you leave London?

London left me. It simply fell out of my soul, but it will return.

As far as I know, you now prefer to live in Paris. What do you like about that city?

Paris is a city I have fallen out of love with. It is far too full of guilt. It is a city where your neighbors are the police. Everyone is a spy, mean, rotten and dirty. I don't like many Parisians. I find them impossible. I now simply lock myself away and work in my atelier – an atelier that sits on top of the Folies Bergère and once belonged to the artist, Kees Van Dongen. I do find, however, Paris attractive, but only as long as I can remain a foreigner. I don't want to speak the language because if I did, I just might kill someone. New York is where I have a life and I spread my time between these two cities. Nevertheless, Paris did show me a certain love for what the English hate and for that, I am deeply grateful. And so, I have to admit, it is on occasion home for me too. I much prefer Baudelaire to Dickens, Guy Debord to Bertrand Russell, Yves Klein to Henry Moore.

Was Paris a point of reference for you even earlier?

Paris is where I discovered how to dream undisturbed. Paris is more than capable of allowing you to do just this. I often find it easy to drift in Paris, turning left when you are supposed to turn right and in doing so, I discover often, something new about myself.

Do you think that Punk in the end did change something on a political level?

Punk gave rise to a new generation of artists. All the YBAs. Punk's politics are the driving force behind a lot of contemporary art. It had a major effect on cultural attitudes. It promoted the amateur over the professional. It slowly began to destroy a culture of desire. Desires that we didn't need. In America, Hip Hop was for me, simply black Punk rock. Punk changed music and fashion. It gave them both a political base to work from – to come together as art as action and that is eternally debated.

Would the world be different without Punk?

Punk made the world then seem innocent, younger, alive. It redefined glamor. It chose to make ugliness appear beautiful. It declared that to be good is boring, so to be bad, is good.

Where would you situate the epicenter of Punk? Was it music, fashion, attitude?

Punk's epicenter was this undeniable feeling of a pre-pubescent child who needs to experience a euphoric sense of pleasure every time he or she screams "Murder!"

In the 19th century Théophile Gautier wrote: "Plutôt la barbarie que l'ennui" (rather barbarism than boredom). Do you think this applies to what Punk initially wanted to achieve?

I and my art school buddies set out to destroy the music industry. We used much of what we had learned and debated in art school to put this into practice. We were cultural terrorists. We believed that the commodification of the culture was something to not just throw stones at or protest but to destroy. We acted like luddites with bows and arrows, defenseless against the juggernaut of a corporate culture hurtling down the motorway at us. We punctured a few tires and occasionally threw one off the road but it was never enough. It was an impossible battle to win but we didn't care. For our old art lecturer told us, "It is better to be a flamboyant failure than any kind of benign success." We polluted life in a way that had never been done before – inventing a new language. It makes contemporary society impossible to exist without it. It is and still remains for corporations the only way to define what is cool. They measure everything against Punk. The politics of boredom was definitely part of it.

When did Punk end?

Punk ended when the same generation put itself up for sale. Punk was never for sale. That was the whole point. There are two words that sum up the culture today. One is authenticity and the other is karaoke. Most artists spend their lives today trying to authenticate a karaoke world but you have to be an alchemist or magician to do that. On the one hand, we live in a karaoke world where everything and everyone is for sale. Looking for the authentic in this world is like looking for a ruby in a field of tin. But there is an increasing thirst for the authentic which when discovered, is usually not for sale.

Or: in what forms does Punk go on living?

It has its own culture inside this world and has unquestionably affected and infected everyone. If we look at contemporary art, it is utterly Punk inspired, whether it be in the form of a marketing phenomenon like Damien Hirst, who had he not become a manufacturer of filthy contemporary art, he would have been a Punk. There are also new contemporaries on the rise like Banksy whose work is simply part of Punk's style. If we look at graphic design nothing compares with the typography of ransom note lettering created by Punk. An extreme luddite form of artistic style and menace that has not ever been surpassed. If we look at fashion, Comme des Garçons, Lanvin, Yves Saint Laurent, Dolce & Gabbana, Louis Vuitton, and a million other labels have all fallen under the spell and dictates of Punk style. The deconstruction of clothes which formed its basis has continued to be the method that most designers choose to make their clothes by. Today's internet culture is an extension of a Punk DIY lifestyle: the blog, facebook, Youtube ... all contribute to this. It is where the cultural terrorist is born today. In fact, it is where most popular culture is made distributed, needing no longer to be servile to and chained by the corporate world. Because of this, corporate culture is having even a harder time today than ever selling the new generation anything. But Punk remains as enigmatic as ever and will continue to live beyond all of our lifetimes as something so wild, so romantic and for the very young, sexier sometimes than sex itself, that it is at the core of all our dreams.

List of Works

Vito Acconci
Born 1940 in New York.
Lives and works in New York.

Under History Lessons, 1976
Painted wood planks, stools, light-bulbs
Approx. 4,8 x 3 x 0,5 m
2-channel audio-CD, 21:25 min.
The Museum of Contemporary Art, Los Angeles. Purchased with funds
provided by the National Endowment for the Arts, a Federal Agency, and
The Broad Art Foundation

Ten Packed Minutes,* 1976
Audio-piece for record compilation
Approx. 12 min.
Courtesy Acconci Studio, New York

Elvira Bach
Born 1951 in Neuenhain, Hessen, Germany.
Lives and works in Berlin.

Sechs Tage Budapest, 1981
Dispersion on paper
6 panels, each 230 x 100 cm
Courtesy the artist and Kaempf Hamburg art & management GmbH

Lynda Benglis
Born 1941 in Lake Charles, Louisiana, USA.
Lives and works in New York and Santa Fe.

Artforum Advertisement, 1974
Iris print
30,5 x 55,9 cm
Courtesy Cheim & Read, New York

Artforum Magazine, Issue November,* 1974
Magazine
33,5 x 55,9 cm
Courtesy Robert Pincus-Witten, New York

Jörg Buttgereit
Born 1963 in Berlin, Germany.
Lives and works in Berlin.

Mein Papi, 1981
Super 8 on DVD
7:10 min.
Courtesy the artist

Die Tödliche Doris
Berlin collective, 1980–1987.

Wolfgang Müller, born 1957 in Wolfsburg, Germany,
lives and works in Berlin und Iceland.
Nikolaus Utermöhlen, born 1958 in Würzburg, Germany,
died 1996 in Berlin.
Käthe Elke Kruse, born 1958 in Westfalen, Germany,
lives and works in Berlin.
Various members: Chris Dreier (1980–1981); Dagmar Dimitroff (1981–
1982); Tabea Blumenschein (1982–1984).

Das Leben des Sid Vicious, 1982
Super 8 on DVD
12 min.
Courtesy Wolfgang Müller

Berliner Küchenmusik, 1982
Super 8 on DVD
5:17 min.
Courtesy Wolfgang Müller

Chöre & Soli, 1983
Miniphon-record with record player, battery and book in box
31,5 cm x 31,5 cm x 5,6 cm
Courtesy Wolfgang Müller

Schmeißt die Krücken weg, 1987
Table out of pressed wood, 2 record players, 2 album covers (*Sechs*,
Unser Debut), poster (84 x 59 cm)
Courtesy Wolfgang Müller

Autogrammkarten '87
Die Schule der Tödlichen Doris, 1987
Dispersion on canvas
8 out of 12, each 18,5 x 12,3 cm
Courtesy Wolfgang Müller

Promotion photograph, Japan-Tour,* 1987
(Photographed at the men's toilet, Bar Kumpelnest 3000, West-Berlin)
Courtesy Wolfgang Müller

Schmuckzahnspange,* 1981/2007
Braces, pearls, wire, jewellery case
Courtesy Wolfgang Müller

Teppichhaarfrisur, 1981/2007
Digital print, passepartout, dark wooden frame
Courtesy Wolfgang Müller

Unser Debut, 1985
Album cover
31 x 31,5 cm
Courtesy Wolfgang Müller

Sechs, 1986
Album cover
31 x 31,5 cm
Courtesy Wolfgang Müller

„ ",* 1981
Album cover
31 x 31,5
Courtesy Wolfgang Müller

Einstürzende Neubauten
West-Berlin Band, founded 1980.

Founder members: Blixa Bargeld, N.U. Unruh, Gudrun Gut, Beate Bartel.
Various artists.

Stahlschlagzeug,* approx. 1980
Blue Bin, 7 Drumsticks, double T-beam, quad percussion, cymbal, steel
snare, bass drum pedal, airconditioningscach, band logo, steel pipe,
sticks, steel bass drum, supermarket trolley
Courtesy rock'n'pop museum, Gronau, Germany

Zeichnungen des Patienten O.T...., 1983
Album cover
31 x 31,5 cm
Courtesy Private Collection

1/2 Mensch, 1985
Album cover
31 x 31,5 cm
Courtesy Private Collection

endart
Berlin collective, based in Kreuzberg West-Berlin, 1980–1988.

god 'n' dog, 1984
Various materials
40 x 26 x 14 cm
Courtesy Private Collection

locus solus, 1983
Acrylic on corrugated cardboard
48 x 40 x 20 cm
Courtesy Private Collection

Venus, 1984
Painted wood, metal, fur
39 x 58 x 27 cm
Courtesy Private Collection

Vagina pectoris, 1984
Painted wood, metal
57 x 25 x 20 cm
Courtesy Private Collection

*Frühstück bei Tiffany,** 1985
b/w photograph
30 x 42 cm
Photo: Dieter Grube
Courtesy Private Collection

Die Geburt eines Igels, 1982
b/w photograph
30 x 42 cm
Photo: Rosi Schäfer
Courtesy Private Collection

Tiergarten, 1985
b/w photograph
21 x 30 cm
Courtesy Private Collection

*Die Idealfrau,** 1984
Painted wood relief
90 x 66 cm
Courtesy Private Collection

*Durch die Wüste Gabi,** 1984
Painted wood relief, 3 parts
41 x 26 / 75 x 73 / 45 x 51 cm
Courtesy Paul Maenz, Berlin

William English
Born in Leicester, England.
Lives and works in London.

Vivienne Westwood, approx. 1975
8 photographs
Each approx. 45,72 x 30,48 cm
Courtesy William English, London

*Vivienne Westwood,** approx. 1975
Giclée print
152 x 120 cm
Courtesy William English, London

Walter Gramming
Born 1952 in Neustadt, Franken, Germany.
Lives and works in Berlin and Ringenwalde, Germany.

Hammer und Sichel, 1978
Super 8 on DVD
4:31 min.
Courtesy the artist

Richard Hambleton
Born 1954 in Vancouver, Canada.
Lives and works in New York.

Shadow Man, 1982
b/w print
50 x 40 cm
Photo: Hank O'Neal
Courtesy Hank O'Neal und Woodward Gallery, New York

Shadow Man, 1982
b/w print
50 x 33,7 cm
Photo: Hank O'Neal
Courtesy Hank O'Neal und Woodward Gallery, New York

Shadow Man, 1982
b/w print
41,6 x 50 cm
Photo: Hank O'Neal
Courtesy Hank O'Neal und Woodward Gallery, New York

Shadow Man, 1982
b/w print
50 x 39 cm
Photo: Hank O'Neal
Courtesy Hank O'Neal und Woodward Gallery, New York

Shadow Man, 1982
b/w print
50 x 49,4 cm
Photo: Hank O'Neal
Courtesy Hank O'Neal und Woodward Gallery, New York

Shadow Man, 1982
b/w print
39,8 x 50 cm
Photo: Hank O'Neal
Courtesy Hank O'Neal und Woodward Gallery, New York

Shadow Man,* 1984
Foamed plastic, acrylic, gel, wire
75,5 x 45,5 x 20 cm
Courtesy ZELLERMAYER Galerie, Berlin

Hormel & Bühler
Dieter Hormel, born 1974 in Göttingen, Germany.
Lives and works in Berlin and Leipzig.

Geld, 1982
Super 8 on DVD
4:10 min.
Courtesy Gudrun Gut

Derek Jarman
Born 1942 in Northwood, Great Britain.
Died 1994 in London.

Jubilee, 1977
Film on DVD
100 min.
Courtesy Whaley-Malin Productions

Manfred Jelinski
Born 1948 in Berlin.
Lives and works in Nordfriesland, Germany.

So war das SO 36,* 1982–1984
Super 8 on DVD
12:02 min.
Courtesy the artist

Richard Kern
Born 1954 in North Carolina, USA.
Lives and works in New York.

Fingered, 1986
Super 8 on DVD
24 min.
Courtesy the artist

Martin Kippenberger
Born 1953 in Dortmund, Germany.
Died 1997 in Vienna, Austria.

Nutzen Sie die ganze Palette unserer Dienstleistungen. Kippenbergers Büro,* 1978
Poster
43 x 30,5 cm
Courtesy Private Collection

This Band is playing on Luxus, 1979
Poster
35,5 x 31, 5 cm
Courtesy Private Collection

This Fellow is playing on Luxus,* 1979
Poster
35,5 x 31,5 cm
Courtesy Private Collection

This Guy is playing on Luxus,* 1979
Poster
35,5 x 31,5 cm
Courtesy Private Collection

This Woman is playing on Luxus,* 1979
Poster
35,5 x 31,5 cm
Courtesy Private Collection

This Man is playing on Luxus, 1979
Poster
35,5 x 31,5 cm
Courtesy Private Collection

SO 36 Veranstaltungsplakat,* 1979
Poster
30 x 30 cm
Courtesy Private Collection

SO 36 Veranstaltungsplakat,* 1979
Poster
38,2 x 30 cm
Courtesy Private Collection

SO 36 Veranstaltungsplakat,* 1979
Poster
43 x 30 cm
Courtesy Private Collection

1/4 Jhdt. Kippenberger als einer von Euch, unter Euch, mit Euch, 1978
Poster
59,5 x 84 cm
Courtesy Private Collection

Linder
Born 1954 in Manchester, Great Britain.
Lives and works in Lancashire, Great Britain.

Untitled, 1977
Collage on paper
35,5 x 38 cm
Courtesy the artist and Stuart Shave/Modern Art, London

Untitled (Buzzcocks Magazine), 1978
Flyer
15 x 20 cm
Courtesy the artist and Stuart Shave/Modern Art, London

Ludus, Concert with Meat Dress, La Hacienda, Manchester, 1982
DVD, 38 min.
Courtesy the artist and Stuart Shave/Modern Art, London

The Secret Public/another music in a different kitchen, 1978
Publication
42 x 30 cm
Courtesy the artist and Stuart Shave/Modern Art, London

Mask I,* 1977
Size variable
Various materials
Courtesy the artist and Stuart Shave/Modern Art, London

Mask II,* 1977
Size variable
Various materials
Courtesy the artist and Stuart Shave/Modern Art, London

*Mask III,** 1977
Size variable
Various materials
Courtesy the artist and Stuart Shave/Modern Art, London

*Untitled (Howard Devoto in mask I),** 1977
Printers proof
39,5 x 50,5 cm
Courtesy the artist and Stuart Shave/Modern Art, London

*Untitled (Howard Devoto in mask II),** 1977
Printers proof
39,5 x 50,5 cm
Courtesy the artist and Stuart Shave/Modern Art, London

Untitled, 1977
Photomontage
51,5 x 41,5 cm
Collection Shane Akeroyd, London

SheShe, 1981
Silver bromide photographs
14 parts, each 74 x 61 cm
Private Collection, London

Untitled, 1977
Photomontage
51,5 x 41,5 cm
Courtesy Paul Stolper, London

Robert Longo
Born in 1953 in New York.
Lives and works in New York.

Joanna, 1983
From the series *Men in the Cities*
Lithograph
182 x 98 cm
ALBERTINA, Vienna

and Larry, 1983
From the series *Men in the Cities*
Lithograph
182 x 98 cm
ALBERTINA, Vienna

Jonathan, 1988
From the series *Men in the Cities*
Lithograph
182 x 98 cm
ALBERTINA, Vienna

Ann Magnuson, Tom Rubnitz
Ann Magnuson, born 1956 in Charleston, West Virginia, USA, lives and
works in New York.
Tom Rubnitz lived and worked in New York, died 1992 in New York.

Made for TV, 1984
Videoperformance
DVD, 15:15 min.
Courtesy Ann Magnuson

Made for TV, 1984
Promotion-Photograph
Photo: Tsen Kwong Chi
Courtesy Ann Magnuson

Malaria!
West-Berlin Band, 1981–1986.
Members: Gudrun Gut, Bettina Köster, Manon Pepita Duursma, Susanne
Kuhnke, Christine Hahn

*Krach durch Freude,** 1979
Flyer
30 x 29 cm
Courtesy Gudrun Gut

Emotion, 1982
Album cover
31 x 31,5 cm
Courtesy Gudrun Gut

*weisses wasser: white water,** 1982
Album cover
31 x 31,5 cm
Courtesy Gudrun Gut

New York Passage, 1982
Album cover
31 x 31,5 cm
Courtesy Gudrun Gut

Untitled, concert and studio shooting,* ca. 1982
2 b/w photos
Each 24 x 17,5 cm
Courtesy Gudrun Gut

*Peppermint Lounge,** 1981
Poster
35,5 x 21,5 cm
Courtesy Gudrun Gut

*Kulturkeller,** 1981
Poster
29 x 21 cm
Courtesy Gudrun Gut

*Untitled,** approx. 1982
Portrait collage
42 x 29 cm
Courtesy Gudrun Gut

Mania D.
West-Berlin Band, 1979–1981
Members: Gudrun Gut, Bettina Köster, Beate Bartel

Summe über Zukunft (also known as Mania D.) in Kippenbergers Büro,*
1979
2 b/w photographs
Each 24 x 17,5 cm
Courtesy Gudrun Gut

Untitled,* 1979
Press photograph, studio
26 x 21 cm
Photo: Jutta Henglein
Courtesy Gudrun Gut

Untitled,* 1979
Draft of album cover
21,5 x 15,5 cm
Courtesy Gudrun Gut

Mania D., *HERZschlag*, 1980
Drawing for single cover
18,5 x 18 cm
Courtesy Gudrun Gut

Untitled,* 1980
Drawing for single cover
Pencil on paper
29 x 21 cm
Courtesy Gudrun Gut

Der Zensor kommt,* ca 1980
Flyer, colour print
14,5 x 21 cm
Courtesy Gudrun Gut

Robert Mapplethorpe
Born 1946 in New York.
Died 1989 in Boston.

Patti Smith, 1976
Gelatin silver print
40,6 x 50,8 cm
Robert Mapplethorpe Foundation, New York

Patti Smith, 1978
Gelatin silver print
40,6 x 50,8 cm
Robert Mapplethorpe Foundation, New York

Patti Smith, 1978
Gelatin silver print
40,6 x 50,8 cm
Robert Mapplethorpe Foundation, New York

Maye & Rendschmidt
Inge Maye, born in Berlin, lives and works in Berlin.
Volker Rendschmidt, born in Berlin, lives and works in Berlin.

Ohne Liebe gibt es keinen Tod, 1980
Super 8 auf DVD
4:28 min.
Courtesy the artists

Mark Morrisroe
Born 1959 in New Maden, Massachusetts, USA.
Died 1989 in New York.

Untitled (La Môme Piaf), 1982
C-print
50,5 x 40,5 cm
Estate Mark Morrisroe (collection Ringier) c/o Photomuseum Winterthur

Untitled (Michael Walsh at home in the kitchen), 1987
C-print
50,5 x 40,5 cm
Estate Mark Morrisroe (collection Ringier) c/o Photomuseum Winterthur

Untitled (self portrait with blue and white wig), approx. 1984
C-print
50,5 x 40,5 cm
Estate Mark Morrisroe (collection Ringier) c/o Photomuseum Winterthur

Untitled (Hello from Bertha), 1983
C-print
40,7 x 50,7 cm
Estate Mark Morrisroe (collection Ringier) c/o Photomuseum Winterthur

Untitled (Jason Skiper on the morning of his father's wedding), 1985
C-print
40,5 x 50,5 cm
Estate Mark Morrisroe (collection Ringier) c/o Photomuseum Winterthur

Untitled, 1982
Gelatin silver print
50,4 x 40,1 cm
Estate Mark Morrisroe (collection Ringier) c/o Photomuseum Winterthur

Untitled
C-print
50,9 x 40,7 cm
Estate Mark Morrisroe (collection Ringier) c/o Photomuseum Winterthur

Untitled
C-print
50,8 x 40,6 cm
Estate Mark Morrisroe (collection Ringier) c/o Photomuseum Winterthur

Notorische Reflexe

Berlin collective, 1982–1986
Members: Sascha von Oertzen, Christoph Doering, Knot Hoffmeister, Gas Twist, Ralf Buron

Fragment Video, 1983
Super 8 on DVD
12:06 min.
Courtesy Christoph Doering

Tony Oursler

Born 1957 in New York.
Lives and works in New York.

The Loner, 1980
Installation, film, sound and props
Dimensions variable
Courtesy the artist and Lisson Gallery, London

Genesis P-Orridge

Born 1950 in Manchester, Great Britain.
Lives and works in New York.

Venus Mount, from *TAMPAX ROMANA*, 1976
Wooden box, broken statue, tampons
30,5 x 30,5 x 15 cm
Courtesy James Birch

It's That Time of the Month, from *TAMPAX ROMANA*, 1976
Wooden box, clock, tampons
30,5 x 30,5 x 15 cm
Courtesy James Birch

Pupae, from *TAMPAX ROMANA*, 1976
Wood, hair, tampons
30,5 x 30,5 x 15 cm
Courtesy James Birch

Jamie Reid

Born 1947 in Croyden, Surrey, Great Britain.
Lives and works in Liverpool.

Sex Pistols, *God Save The Queen*,1976
Single cover
18,5 x 18 cm
Courtesy Private Collection

Sex Pistols, *Anarchy In The U.K.,* 1976
Single cover
18,5 x 18 cm
Courtesy Private Collection

Sex Pistols, *Never Mind The Bollocks Here's The Sex Pistols*, 1977
Album cover
31 x 31,5 cm
Courtesy Private Collection

Sex Pistols, *Holidays In The Sun*, 1977
Single cover
18,5 x 18 cm
Courtesy Private Collection

God Save The Queen,* 1976
Printers proof
Stolper/Wilson Collection, London

Holidays In The Sun Sex Pistols,* 1977
Poster
Approx. 70 x 100 cm
Stolper/Wilson Collection, London

Never Mind The Bollocks,* 1977
Poster
Approx. 70 x 100 cm
Courtesy Stolper/Wilson Collection, London

The Great Rock 'n' Roll Swindle, *1979
Rotten bar
Approx. 55 x 38 cm
Collection Jon Savage

Anarchy In The U.K.,* 1976
Poster
Approx. 55 x 38 cm
Collection Jon Savage

God Save The Queen,* 1977
Cover draft
Approx. 55 x 38 cm
Collection Jon Savage

Two Boredom Buses,* 1976
Poster
Approx. 55 x 38 cm
Collection Jon Savage

Jamie Reid, Sophie Richmond, Vivienne Westwood

Anarchy in the U.K. Sex Pistols, No. 1, 1976
Fanzine
Stolper/Wilson Collection, London

Johnny Rozsa

Born 1949 in the USA.
Lives and works in New York.

Leigh Bowery

Born 1961 in Melbourne, Australia.
Died 1994 in London.

Leigh Bowery with Trojan, Pakis from Outer Space, 1983
C-print
50 x 50 cm
Courtesy Johnny Rozsa, New York

Leigh Bowery with Trojan, Pakis from Outer Space, 1983
C-print
50 x 50 cm
Courtesy Johnny Rozsa, New York

Steve Strange, 1984
Baryt-print
50 x 50 cm
Courtesy Johnny Rozsa, New York

Marilyn, 1984
Baryt-print
50 x 50 cm
Courtesy Johnny Rozsa, New York

Boy George, 1978
Baryt-print
50 x 50 cm
Courtesy Johnny Rozsa, New York

Christy Rupp
Born in New York.
Lives and works in New York.

The Rat Patrol, New York, 1979
b/w photograph
10 x 15 cm
Courtesy the artist

Rat Patrol, 1979
5 posters
Each 15 x 45 cm
Courtesy the artist

Salomé
Salomé aka Wolfgang Ludwig Cihlarz born 1954 in Karlsruhe, Germany.
Lives and works in Berlin.

Fuck 1, 1977
Acrylic on nettle
160 x 210 cm
Collection Salomé, Berlin
Courtesy Galerie Deschler, Berlin

Geile Tiere,* 1982
Album cover
31 x 31,5 cm
Collection Salomé, Berlin

Geile Tiere,* 1980
2 single covers
Each 18,5 x 18 cm
Collection Salomé, Berlin

Salomé & Luciano Castelli
Luciano Castelli born 1951 in Luzern, Switzerland.
Lives and works in Paris.

Rote Liebe, 1979
Acrylic on nettle
240 x 400 cm
Collection Salomé, Berlin
Courtesy Galerie Deschler, Berlin

Jon Savage
Born 1953 in England.
Lives and works in London.

Untitled (London), 1977
10 b/w photographs
Each 55 x 38 cm
Courtesy the artist

Alan Vega aka Alan Suicide
Born 1948 in Brooklyn, New York.
Lives and works in New York.

Alan Suicide, American Supreme 2, 1976/2001
Mixed Media
Dimensions variable
Courtesy the artist and Deitch Projects, New York

Alan Suicide, Alien,* 1976/2001
Mixed Media
116,8 x 60,9 cm
Courtesy the artist and Deitch Projects, New York

Arturo Vega
Born in Mexico.
Lives and works in New York.

Silver Dollar, 1973
b/w print on canvas
152 x 203 cm
Collection of Ramonesworld.com

Ramones Logo, 1976
Colour print
27,9 x 43,2 cm
Collection of Ramonesworld.com

Ramones Classic Logo,* 1977
Colour print
27,9 x 43,2 cm
Collection of Ramonesworld.com

Rocket to Russia Logo,* 1977
Colour print
27,9 x 43,2 cm
Collection of Ramonesworld.com

Ramones Poster, 1975
Poster
48,5 x 36,8 cm
Collection of Ramonesworld.com

Ramones Eagle (backdrop and light work), 1977–89
Colour print
20,3 x 25,4 cm
Collection of Ramonesworld.com

Ramones first album,* 1976
Album cover
31 x 31,5 cm
Collection of Ramonesworld.com

Ramones,* 1974
8 b/w photographs
Collection of Ramonesworld.com

Vivienne Westwood
Born 1941 in Glossop, Derbyshire, Great Britain.
Lives and works in London.

Black Bondage Coat,* approx. 1976
Courtesy Vivienne Westwood Archive

Purple Mules,* approx. 1974
Courtesy Murray Blewett

Black Pants,* approx. 1974
Courtesy Vivienne Westwood Archive

Vivienne Westwood & Malcolm McLaren
Malcolm McLaren, born 1946 in London, lives and works in New York and Paris.

Two Cowboys,* approx. 1976
T-shirt
Stolper/Wilson Collection, London

Rape,* approx. 1976
T-shirt
Stolper/Wilson Collection, London

Mickey & Minnie,* approx. 1976
Mini dress
Stolper/Wilson Collection, London

Destroy,* approx. 1976
T-shirt
Stolper/Wilson Collection, London

Vivienne Westwood & Malcolm McLaren & Bernie Rhodes
You're gonna wake up in the morning,* approx. 1976
T-shirt
Stolper/Wilson Collection, London

Stephen Willats
Born 1943 in London.
Lives and works in London.

Model Dwellings, 1982
Photo print, acrylic, pen, letraset text and objects on paper and cardboard
2 panels, each 90 x 144 cm
Courtesy the artist and Gallery Christian Nagel, Köln, Germany

David Wojnarowicz
Born 1954 in New Jersey.
Died 1992 in New York

Arthur Rimbaud in New York, 1978–79/2004
12 gelatin silver prints out of 44
Each 27,5 x 35,5 cm
Courtesy Cabinet London, PPOW Gallery, New York and The Estate of David Wojnarowicz

Heroin, 1979
Super 8 on DVD, 3 min., silent
Courtesy Fales Library, New York University

Wolkenstein & Markgraf
Rolf S. Wolkenstein, born 1958 in Stuttgart, lives and works in Berlin.
Horst Markgraf, born in Stuttgart, lives and works in Berlin.

Hüpfen 82, 1982
Super 8 on DVD
2:15 min.
Courtesy the artists

Bill Woodrow
Born 1948 in Oxfordshire, Great Britain.
Lives and works in London.

Car Door, Armchair and Incident, 1981
Car door, armchair, enamel paint
120 x 300 x 300 cm
Courtesy the artist and Waddington Galleries, London

Cerith Wyn Evans
Born 1958 in Llanelli, Great Britain.
Lives and works in London.

Epiphany, 1984
16 mm film on DVD
24 min.
Courtesy the artist und Jay Jopling/ White Cube, London

Yana Yo
Born 1959 in Wimbern, Germany.
Lives and works in Cologne.

Sax, 1983
Super 8 on DVD
5:47 min.
Courtesy the artist

Furthermore

Ielevision at CBGB,* 1974
Poster
55,8 x 38,1 cm
Courtesy Jon Savage

Patti Smith and Television at CBGB,* 1975
Poster
55,8 x 38,1 cm
Courtesy Jon Savage

DIN A Testbild
Programm 1, 1980
Album cover
31 x 31,5 cm
Courtesy Private Collection

The Clash
London Calling, 1979
Album cover
31 x 31,5 cm
Courtesy Private Collection

No New York, 1978
Album cover
31 x 31,5 cm
Courtesy Private Collection

The Clash
The Clash, 1977
Album cover
31 x 31,5 cm
Courtesy Private Collection

Throbbing Gristle
T.G., 1977
Album cover
31 x 31,5 cm
Courtesy Private Collection

X-Ray Spex
Germfree Adolescents, 1978
Album cover
31 x 31,5 cm
Courtesy Private Collection

Talking Heads
77, 1977
Album cover
31 x 31,5 cm
Courtesy Private Collection

Talking Heads
More Songs About Buildings and Food, 1978
Album cover
31 x 31,5 cm
Courtesy Private Collection

New York Dolls
Too much too soon, 1974
Album cover
31 x 31,5 cm
Courtesy Private Collection

Blondie
Blondie, 1976
Album cover
31 x 31,5 cm
Courtesy Private Collection

Contortions
Buy, 1979
Album cover
31 x 31,5 cm
Courtesy Private Collection

James White and The Blacks
off white, 1979
Album cover
31 x 31,5 cm
Courtesy Private Collection

Lydia Lunch
Queen of Siam, 1979
Album cover
31 x 31,5 cm
Courtesy Private Collection

Ramones
Rocket to Russia, 1977
Album cover
31 x 31,5 cm
Courtesy Private Collection

Several important items have been borrowed from 'England's Dreaming:
The Jon Savage Archive' held at Liverpool John Moores University, which
are not on the list of works. *
'England's Dreaming: The Jon Savage Archive' is the biggest single
central source of Punk-related material in the world. Jon Savage is
one of the UK's leading cultural historians and the archive contains
the resources collected by him for his seminal research and writing.
The archive consists of mainly print material and is currently housed
in 26 boxes. Most of the five thousand plus items are from Britain,
but there are many examples from Europe and America. As well as
photographs by most of the name photographers of the day, there are
fanzines, individually produced fan magazines, from Britain and America,
including a complete set of the first Punk fanzine, Sniffin' Glue. There is a
collection of interviews with leading figures of the Punk scene (including
musicians and artists). The archive also contains a considerable amount
of documentation about the Sex Pistols, ranging from handbills to press
clippings and photographs.
The England's Dreaming Archive is the archive of England's Dreaming:
Sex Pistols and Punk Rock, the book written by Jon Savage now
regarded as the definitive account of Punk Rock and British society in the
mid to late 1970's. England's Dreaming tells the story of Punk and Britain
in the late 1970's through the brief rise and fall of the Sex Pistols. Over
the sixteen years since its first publication in 1991, England's Dreaming
has sold over 100,000 copies, and has seen editions in America, France,
Germany, Italy, Japan and China. It was re-promoted in a second edition
in the United Kingdom during 2002, and was republished in Spring 2005
in a third edition.
Punk Rock was not just a music/style phenomenon but a national issue,
and the archive reflects this. Contextual material for the time is also
provided by many national newspapers and magazines, as well as many
editions of the weekly music press. This unmatched archive presents a
unique opportunity to examine further a hotly contested period that is
now recognised as a crucial point in British 20th century history.
Consultant: Professor Colin Fallows

The exhibition includes a large amount of further historical artefacts such
as record sleeves, manifestos, and photographic documentation, which
are not on the list of works.*

* Exhibits with no image in the catalogue